Conversations With

Ann Howard

Susan Higgins

Conversations With
Ann Howard

by Susan Higgins

AuthorHouse™ UK Ltd.
1663 Liberty Drive
Bloomington, IN 47403 USA
www.authorhouse.co.uk
Phone: 0800.197.4150

Published by AuthorHouse 01/14/2013

ISBN: 978-1-4918-8118-7 (sc)
978-1-4918-8119-4 (e)

All the photographs in this book are from Miss Ann Howard's personal collection. The photographers,
where possible, have been credited and their permission sought to illustrate this biography.

The author wishes to sincerely thank a number of people who have advised, edited and corrected the script of this
book: Graeme Kay, James Lockhart, Tom Higgins, Alison Sutherland, Vittoria Telo and Ann herself.

This book is printed on acid-free paper.

authorHOUSE®

Foreword
A Greeting From Ann

Why did I want this book to be written?

Well, I think I have had a very happy life, I've made friends, some as far back as 60 years when I was in my amateur opera days and some from my professional life. Naturally things change as you get older, but luckily, reading through my diaries it all comes flooding back. I hope, dear readers, you will enjoy all this.

Acknowledgments

My first thanks must go to Ann herself, who generously gave me many hours of her time to willingly describe her life and career; also to let me see, and have the use of her photographs.

I received much valuable advice from Vittoria Telo about the book design and production.

Tom Higgins suggested the title and has given me much encouragement—as has Michael Letchford who has, himself, written biographies of the famous singers Terese Malton and Walter Widdup. James Lockhart corrected many details of the opera world. My thanks also goes to Graeme Kay for editorial consultancy and to Alison Sutherland for proof reading it. A number of photographers were generous enough to allow me to use their pictures free of charge and others for discounted fees. The photographs and pictures were expertly scanned by Karim Al Sayegh

Contents

The Gypsy Baron/J. Strauss; *La bohème*/Puccini; *Hansel and Gretel*/Humperdinck; *Oedipus Rex*/Stravinsky; *L'heure Espagnole*/Ravel

Die Walküre/Wagner; The *Mines of Sulphur*/Bennett; *Samson and Delilah*/Saint-Saëns (also in subsequent chapters); *The Trojans*/Berlioz; *Iolanthe*/Gilbert and Sullivan; *The Arcadians*/ Monckton; *The Rake's Progress*/ Stravinsky; *Ariadne auf Naxos*/R.Strauss; *Rusalka*/Dvořák (also Chapter 9); *Cendrillon*/Massenet; The *Valkyrie*/Wagner; *The Mock doctor*/Gounod; *Orfeo*/Monteverdi; *Mavra*/Stravinsky; *Bluebeard*/Offenbach;

Carmen/Bizet (and subsequent chapters); *Kiss Me Kate*/Cole Porter; *Osud*/Janáček; *Lohengrin*/Wagner; *Aïda*/Verdi; *Tristan and Isolde*/Wagner; *The Rhinegold*/Wagner; *Katya Kabanova*/Janáček; *La traviata*/ Verdi; *Arden Must Die*/Goehr; *War and Peace*/Prokofiev (also chapter 9); *Armide*/Gluck; *La Grande Duchesse de Gerolstein*/Offenbach(also chapter 9); *L'Egisto*/Cavalli; *The Italian Girl in Algiers*/Rossini; *The Force of Destiny*/Verdi; The *Consul*/Menotti; *Don Carlos*/Verdi;

CHAPTER 1

'I Shall Go On The Stage'

May 6th 2011

Sitting in her pleasant home in Surbiton, looking out at a lovely, tree-lined garden, I turned on my tape-recorder for the first time to record the life-journey of Ann Howard. Her name, and the memories of her many leading roles in opera are familiar with the opera-going public both here in London and in many opera houses across the world. As we search through her diaries and she recalls her experiences, I realize that her career coincided with the start of English National, Welsh National and Scottish Operas and the great popularity that opera then began to enjoy in this country.

Now opera was not to be just for the 'toffs' and we could hear it sung in our own language. Even the World Cup featured an opera aria – Puccini's 'Nessun Dorma' – which went on to be hugely popular. (Bless you Pavarotti). Famous operas got a facelift, modern composers wrote new operas and thousands of people discovered opera for the first time – and loved it. During these years from the 1960s onwards, Ann's career steadily grew.

What I was not to know on this first day was that my research into her life and career would be in three stages: this first stage when she recounted her experiences and we searched through all her appointment diaries; then many hours riffling through some deep drawers where there was a wealth of photographs; and finally to gain access to the many press reviews that she acquired, all of which had been faithfully collected by Keith, her husband.

Each stage was fascinating. The story of Ann's emergence from being a shop assistant to an opera diva reads almost like a fairy story, and the ensuing years of work paint a daunting picture of an opera singer's life. The photographs suddenly brought all this to life; here was the glamour, the wonderful costumes and make-up, the interesting and often famous colleagues that she worked with, and above all the indisputable evidence of her considerable beauty.

The press reports give yet another view of her career, and collectively they build up a very good idea of the actual opera productions and Ann's interpretations of her roles. They also describe the audience's reactions, and of course, the reactions of the reviewers – who were often so overwhelmed by her beauty, sexuality and stage presence that they almost forgot to mention her magnificent voice and fine singing.

I mentioned the discovery of the press reviews to a fellow author who advised me to put in the bad ones as well as the good; however, bad reviews were virtually non-existent. Of course, when she played minor roles the press didn't waste newsprint on her, but gave her one sentence or possibly damned her with faint praise; but when she emerged in principal roles – notably when she sang Carmen – she received rave reviews.

Her very first thought was that she wanted this biography to be a fun book, not just a recital of all her triumphs. I later realised that this attitude reflected the essentially modest approach to her success. She glories more in the happy memories of working with great people rather than accepting accolades herself. From the very beginning she brought an amateur's enthusiasm to her work – while being a consummate professional.

So where did it all begin? Certainly not by having music lessons at school or having a musical home life.

The 'Dear little thing'

It was in her Junior school in Norwood, South London, that Ann Howard first performed to the public, albeit only to her classmates. She has recollections that she was considered 'a dear little thing' and was taken from classroom to classroom to sing 'There's not a tint that paints the rose'.

At the age of six and seven her favourite song was 'Ragtime Cowboy Jo'. 'I have always been singing and performing,' she said. She had no fear of performing and adored all the glamorous musical films of Ginger Rogers and Fred Astaire. She knew, even then, that this is what she wanted to do herself. At the age of 12 or 13 she had some early singing lessons from a Miss Pauly who also put on some little concerts.

She moved on to a Middle school, and it was a teacher there (actually one who tried, not entirely successfully, to teach Ann shorthand and typing) who introduced her into an amateur operatic society in London called 'The Geoids'. She was to remain a member of this society for many years. However, at this point she was only 14 years old and was not permitted to sing with them until her next birthday.

Did she learn as a schoolgirl the art of getting on with people and how to co-operate in a group? If she did, it augured well for her in her future life of working in an operatic company. Was her school particularly musical? It was a school that aimed to turn out efficient office workers, and Ann showed little talent or interest in this. Her school folder had the wonderfully misspelt title of 'Bookeeping' and she was the despair of her teachers. She confesses that her interests in school were art, English and netball – no mention of music. No, it was to be the heady theatrical atmosphere of the operatic society that made her vow ' I shall go on the stage'. She wrote these prophetic words in her diary just before she left school.

Ann's 15th birthday came at the end of the school year, 1949. Her mother, at this point, took charge of Ann's life. Ann is quick to say that this would be unlikely to happen nowadays, but at the time she was quite happy to be taken from school and, without any summer holiday, found a job in London. In fact she had a series of jobs, the first being with a wholesale textile firm called 'Cooks of St Paul's', situated right next to St Paul's cathedral in London. She stayed there for one year. Her work included modelling garments for the buyers of high street stores. Modestly, she does not put this down to her obviously fine figure, but to the fact that she is 5 foot 10 inches tall. Also, now being the magic age of 15, she was able to be in a show with the Geoids. It was to be Edward German's *Merrie England*. Her first stage experience.

'Merrie England' – Ann with husband-to-be Keith Giles, in the Geoid company
Photo: K.J.Pugh

At the end of the year, her mother said 'Come on Pauline, we'll find you another job.' Pauline is Ann's second name by which she was known by all of her family. She was Pauline Swadling.

This second job was with Finnigans of Bond Street, a very high class jewellery shop that also sold luxury goods like hand bags. Naturally it had a high class clientele. Ann smiled as she recounted how she nearly knocked over a small man who turned out to be the Duke of Windsor. She apologised profusely of course, and he was very gracious. She also remembers the great excitement of seeing John Wayne standing on the pavement opposite the shop, resplendent in a white suit, set off with a white Stetson. She felt that she was rubbing shoulders with the celebrities of the time.

She remained in the jewellery department for a year, after which her mother again took charge, this time finding her a job with what was then known as 'The Goldsmiths and Silversmiths Company' at 112, Regent Street – later known as Garrards, the Crown Jewellers. It was a magnificent shop into which many famous and celebrated people came. She remembers seeing Elizabeth Taylor and Michael Wilding and many other famous people. Ann was thrilled to be so close to such glitterati.

Ann recalls a number of adventures that she had in the watch and clock department where she was put to work. Describing herself as 'my usual clumsy self', she received an extremely valuable old clock from a customer for repairs and took down all the details. Happily the customer then left the shop as Ann picked it up by the handle at the top which duly parted company with the body of the clock and crashed on to the counter. 'It didn't break the counter,' she said. But it didn't do the clock much good'.

Another terrible adventure was with a fabulous, hand-made watch which came in for a minor adjustment. It was usual for these small jobs to be done on the spot by a watchmaker. Ann took the watch to the place where the repairs took place, but the watchmaker was not there. With breathtaking – but misplaced – confidence Ann decided to do the adjustment herself. She took the knife that was used to open watches, sliced it across the back of the watch, and cut off the button and the stem. With a ten-thousand pound damaged watch in her hand the manager appeared.

It could have been what is nowadays popularly known as a 'pivotal moment'. However, without a word the manager went back to the customer. 'I'm sorry sir,' he said. 'Much more difficult job than we ever thought. The watch will have to go back to Switzerland. [Which it did.] Look in our cases and pick another watch until yours is returned.'

How did Ann survive these – and many other – incidents? Perhaps because she was an attractive 'front-of-house' receptionist, but more likely because she had become a member of Garrard's operatic society and was already well-known as a good singer. The rest of the staff called her their 'Nightingale'.

Throughout these first years of working Ann had acquired some amateur stage experience and was having voice lessons, at first with a well-known concert singer called Topliss Green. She then studied with Madame Rudolpha Lhombino who lived on Kingston Hill and with whom she remained for some years.

Early Gilbert and Sullivan productions for the Geoid company

Top: 'Princess Ida

Lower left: 'Iolanthe' — Ann in the role of Phyllis, an Arcadian

Shepherdess

Upper right: 'Patience'

Ann, aged 17, in pre-professional days with the Argennon Amateur Operatic Society (Garrard's own company) in a production of 'Stand Up & Sing'

With the Garrard company she remembers doing a 1930s show called *Stand Up & Sing* which had originally starred Jack Buchanan and Elsie Randolph. Ann had a glamorous, but comic part of 'The Princess'. 'That was rather fun' she remembered. What happened next she describes as 'the most important day in my career.'

Ann often chatted to the customers at Garrards and one day an elderly man came in. She started talking about shows and singing. She was 17 years old at this point, and was a member of both the Garrards operatic society and the Geoids Society. It probably didn't take much prompting for her to enthuse about all this.

The gentleman told her that he was putting on a show, and would she like to come and sing for him? Ann had no idea who he was, and probably suspected that he ran another amateur company somewhere. However, she readily agreed. She then discovered that he was a well-known theatrical producer from pre-war days – Jack Waller.

When Waller next came into Garrards he told Ann that he was putting on a show called *Wild Grows The Heather* the musical version of J.M.Barrie's *The Little Minister*, and was having auditions at the Strand Theatre.

At this point, two important strands of Ann's life came together: her singing career and her married life. She was newly-married to Keith Giles whom she had met at amateur rehearsals. They married in 1954 when she was 19 years old. Keith was a fine amateur pianist who had studied at the Royal College of Music in London.

Ann with producer Jack Waller Photo: Associated Newspapers Ltd.

Wedding bells for Ann and Keith

Ann with her parents, William and Winifred Swadling

Ann and Keith entertain on a cruise ship

The couple went to the Strand Theatre and, unlike all the other interviewees, Ann sang an impressive modern song (with a fiendish accompaniment for Keith) called 'Love Went A-Riding' by Frank Bridge. History doesn't tell us how this audition went, but the result was dramatic. Jack Waller immediately walked up to the stage and said that they would like Ann in the show. However, there was no part for her. (Ann said that she had no idea that that was his intention) – but that he would write her the title song: 'Wild Grows The Heather'. This was quite staggering, life-changing news for her. She left Garrards and began rehearsals as a professional singer. The show opened in Manchester – the first of many journeys outside of London.

Ann, right, stands outside the Palace Theatre in Manchester where she first performed professionally

CHAPTER 2

Principal Boy

What was Ann's voice like at this time? She said that it ranged from soprano to mezzo soprano. She claims that all female voices start off as sopranos. Clearly, at this point it was ideal for show songs. We should perhaps thank her teacher, Madame Lhombino, for carefully guarding her young voice from unnecessary strain. Many promising singers fall at the first hurdle by over singing and using the voice incorrectly. However, it must also have been Ann's ability to use the stage and her statuesque figure that gave her a measure of success at this time. She also had a guardian in the form of her husband who must have protected her against some of the social pitfalls of the theatrical world as well as helping her to learn songs. The Manchester show was produced by Ralph Reader and the music director was – and here Ann paused in her account of this adventure – Geraldo. ' Amazing'. She rehearsed the specially-written title song 'Wild Grows the Heather' and sang it at a performance in Edinburgh. She was already 'on the road'.

The show opened at the Hippodrome in London. It was not a huge success. It was an old-fashioned musical done in an old-fashioned way and this was the time of *West Side Story* which was totally different. But no bones were broken and it had served to set her on her theatrical career. Jack Waller said that Ann should now go into pantomime and that she should sing for Gwladlys Stanley, a lady who owned the Alhambra, Bradford and the Theatre Royal in Leeds. Ann assured him that she knew nothing about pantomime, but Waller saw this as a good career move for her. He arranged for her to be seen on stage by Ms. Stanley who had, in fact, already seen Ann in *Wild Grows the Heather*, singing her special song and looking pretty with the chorus.

Ms. Stanley at first assumed that she could be a principal girl, but Waller knew that she was far too tall for that part. He told Ann to go on stage in a costume that would suggest a principal boy. This astounded her, but she played along with it, getting into tights, muttering to herself 'This is ridiculous'.

Gwladlys Stanley had been a famous principal boy in her time and she was very happy to use Ann in that role. She gave Ann a lot of attention, finding her different costumes for each scene. The pantomime' *Queen of Hearts'* opened in Leeds.

First morning call. Front row: Ann, Eddie Henderson, Gwladys Stanley Laidler, Jimmy Page and Mary Millar
Photo: The Yorkshire Post

Ann in her first pantomime — Queen of Hearts — for Gwladys Stanly Laidler in Leeds

Ann has little recollection as to what she sang, but, unlike pantomime today, her songs were not 'pop' songs, but 'straight' ballads. Without doubt this was a wonderful training ground in stagecraft. After this pantomime she was head-hunted by a more illustrious company, Howard and Wyndham, which owned theatres in Aberdeen, Glasgow and Newcastle. She was offered more money. Ann did four years of pantomime during which she worked with Tommy Steele in Liverpool ('a nice man'). During the summer she occasionally sang for Radio Luxemburg in the *Eddie Calvert Show*. The decision was then made to change course.

Ann with Tommy Steele in the Howard & Wyndham pantomime 'Goldilocks and the Three Bears
Photo: Record Mirror

Pantomime images:
'High, wide and handsome': the opening number of 'Goody Two Shoes' 1959/60 at the Alhambra, Glasgow

Act 2. 'Goody's bedroom: 'Love Walked In'

Keith felt that her developing voice was too good for pantomime and arranged for her to audition for the musical stage. She got the second cover for Eliza Doolittle at the Theatre Royal, Drury Lane and was even given the costume for the part. The first cover was Ann Rogers. However, Ann was still under contract to Howard and Wyndham and they wouldn't release her. Perhaps at the time she was disappointed by this, but she realised later on that, had she gone on to the West End stage, her career might have been completely different. She loved the musical stage – still does to this day – but the opera world would have been without one of its greatest mezzo sopranos if she had stayed there. She worked out her contract with Howard and Wyndham and was ready for the next stage.

Publicity photograph for front of house at the Alhambra Theatre, Glasgow 1959
Photo: Landseer (London)

Ann now had the professional name of Ann Howard – given to her by Jack Waller. Other possible names were Pauline Swadling; Ann Giles; Ann Swadling; and others that were nearer to her real name. These were rejected. The name Howard gave her a few problems in Scotland as it is a Scottish name and there she was assumed to be Scottish.

CHAPTER 3

Opera At Last

Ann as Carmen   Photo: Ken Howard 1975 Santa Fe

In 1959 Keith wrote to the Royal Opera House, Covent Garden to request an audition for Ann. At this time Ann had had no experience of opera – in fact she had only been once to see an opera: *Rusalka* at Sadler's Wells with Joan Hammond in the leading role. She also remembers seeing the film version of *Aïda* with Sophia Loren and being taken to Covent Garden to hear Gertrud Grob-Prandl sing *Turandot* (of which she has no particular memories.) This hardly amounted to a knowledge of opera. She leared, no doubt with Keith's help, the famous aria from *Aïda* 'Ritorna Vincitor' and sang it at the first of five auditions for The Royal Opera in a slow, Wagnerian style. After she had sung, the music director said 'You made it very difficult for yourself, didn't you. It is terribly difficult to sing it at that slow speed.' Doubtless though, the slow tempo served to show off her voice.

Ann had insisted that she was applying for a place in the chorus of the opera, and had stated so at the auditions. This she was given. She certainly had no thoughts about being a principal singer as her knowledge of opera was so slim. However, much later on she was told that the Royal Opera would have offered her a minor principal contract. She remained in the chorus for three years as a second soprano. There could be few better training grounds. She was also still continuing to have singing lessons with Madame Llombino in Kingston.

The conductor Edward Downes approached her and said that he would like her to audition on the stage of Covent Garden. She didn't ask why and chose 'Dich teure Halle' from Wagner's *Tannhäuser* – a fiendish aria with a high B natural. Sometime later Ann remembers hearing Downes running up some stairs to her dressing room saying' 'you've got, you've got it.' 'What?' she asked. 'The American "Astor" money to study singing.' This award was made by a wealthy American, Mrs Vincent Astor, to show her appreciation of the English music critic, Francis Toye.

Considerably astonished, Ann went to see Sir David Webster, the General Administrator of the Royal Opera House, who informed Ann that she was to study with Maestro Dominic Modesti in Paris – who, he felt, would be ideal for her voice.

CHAPTER 4

'A Paris'

In Paris: Dominic Modesti with some of his students

Her first thought was that she couldn't possibly go to Paris. She said as much to Keith, but here again her personal and professional life came together in a most satisfactory way. Keith said that they would both go to Paris – that he would give up his job and accompany her. They moved to what she describes as a 'strange' hotel in Montmartre.

The scholarship was for six months to have daily lessons with Modesti. Five lessons a week. It was very intensive. The lesson would commence with 20 minutes of exercises, and then Keith would come in and work with her on the roles that she was studying . In the afternoon the Salle Pleyel Studios were made available for her to practise. With Keith, she was able to prepare for each lesson. With this schedule they had little time to enjoy Paris as tourists, and as the bursary was only for Ann, there was very little money to spare. She remembers fixing one-pot meals in the hotel room.

It was with Modesti that she worked on her dramatic soprano range. He was convinced, at this stage, that she was a soprano. She learned the role of Sieglinde from Wagner's opera *Die Walküre* and many of the famous soprano arias from the soprano repertoire. However, Ann felt, even then, that she was not 'a real' soprano. She commented that a high mezzo voice can often sing soprano arias, though would not be able to sustain a whole role with all the usual duets and ensembles. It was to be some years later that she finally felt settled as a high mezzo.

Singing has its own unique problems. Everyone who starts to study voice production has a different range of skills and defects to cope with. Learning to sing is unlike other musical study: the difficulties of playing a musical instrument are very apparent and there are numerous books of studies that can be utilized. I asked Ann to tell me more about these lessons. What exercises did he give her – how did he approach the upper and lower ranges of her voice – did he have any special thoughts on breath control?

Ann's first recollection of Modesti's methods was that he had a wonderfully simple way of telling her how to sing which she found instantly understandable. Unlike many singing teachers who go into often confusing details of anatomy and physiology, he gave her a few exercises to 'place' the voice in the optimum way to produce a clear sound that can carry. This is sometimes described as 'putting an edge on the voice'. In exercises that stretched the voice from high to low she learnt to place the voice 'high' for the low notes and 'lower' for the high notes – seemingly the opposite to what would be the natural thing to do – but this avoided having a 'woolly' lower range or a harsh upper range. 'You just drop the jaw and place the voice,' she said. 'None of this fancy business that it goes up round your head and out through your ear or something!'. (Definitely a 'no nonsense' approach.) The technique concentrates the voice tone and gives it natural amplification without wear and tear on the larynx. She has used Modesti's exercises throughout her whole career and now teaches them to her pupils.

Ann and Keith returned to England and she continued her career with the Royal Opera at Covent Garden. She found that much had changed in her absence. Notably, Georg Solti had arrived as Music Director and Joan Ingpen was in charge of casting. Ann was given a series of small roles: the Dama in Verdi's *Macbeth* – which was a very high part, then a Valkyrie which was for a medium voice. She covered the part of one of the Rhinemaidens, (she remembers that one of the other maidens was Kiri te Kanawa), and she sang the role of Kate Pinkerton in Puccini's *Madama Butterfly*.

Perhaps she would have remained as a minor principal singer at Covent Garden for the rest of her career. Indeed, she was very happy doing so. However, Keith felt that she should be looking elsewhere for bigger roles. Ann admits that she was not particularly ambitious and was happy to continue as things were. Keith was the moving force behind her emerging career. He arranged for her to audition for Sadler's Wells Opera.

CHAPTER 5

New, And Bigger Roles At Sadlers Wells

Ann as Czypra, the Gipsy Queen in 'The Gipsy Baron' by Johann Strauss; her first role with Sadler's Wells Opera 1964/5
Photo: Houston Rogers

When she arrived at Sadler's Wells they asked her if she knew the second aria in *Samson and Delilah* 'Amour, viens aider ma faiblesse' ('Love, come to my aid'). 'Oh yes' she confidently said. (In fact she didn't know it at all.) 'Come back and sing it to us next week then'.

Ann describes this aria as 'fabulous' – and very difficult with an enormous range. She – with Keith's invaluable help – must have worked very hard to prepare it for the audition. It was successful and she was invited to join the company.

At this time Sadler's Wells Opera was formed by two companies called individually the 'S' company and the 'W' company. One of these would be on tour throughout Britain while the other gave regular performances at Sadler's Wells theatre in Islington. As a principal singer, Ann worked with both companies – often simultaneously.

The first role that she undertook was the Gypsy Queen in Johann Strauss's opera *The Gypsy Baron* conducted by VilemTausky. This part was an older woman – (her daughter in the opera was sung by June Bronhill who was in fact older than Ann.) Ann commented that, because of her voice type, she often sang the roles of older women. This meant that ,later in her career, when she was indeed rather older, she could still play the same roles; unlike high sopranos who almost inevitably had young girl roles. She also undertook the role of Musetta in Puccini's opera *La bohème* and was establishing herself as a high mezzo soprano, able to sing up to a high B natural, but with a powerful lower range. She was coming towards the end of her twenties, her voice and her stage skills developing all the time while undertaking very diverse roles.

PRESS

<u>Gipsy Baron by Johann Strauss. Sadler's Wells production 1965 conducted by Vilem Tausky</u>

ANN HOWARD brought warmth with her ample tones to the part of the gipsy Czipra

D.A.W.M.—DAILY TELEGRAPH May 27 1965

Vilem Tausky, the conductor, deftly phrases the sighs as well as the smiles in the music; ANN HOWARD, as the Gipsy woman Czipra, and June BronhilL as her daughter, Saffi, are perfectly convincing.

OBSERVER JUNE 14 1964

The old Gipsy Queen is strongly impersonated by Miss ANN HOWARD, a mezzo of genuine accomplishments (though she looks ridiculously young for the role)

Music Critic—THE TIMES June 10 1964

ANN HOWARD as the gipsy woman, Czipra, was splendidly secure and exact vocally, but her acting was hardly helped by her rummage-sale costume, like a swagger coat in ancient sacking.

Edward Greenfield—THE GUARDIAN June 10 1964

Now a principal singer, Ann received her first review from the press. These were not very encouraging to start with, though her dominant presence on the stage was acknowledged form the start.

PRESS

La bohème by Giacomo Puccini Sadler's Wells 1966

ANN HOWARD brought the house down with her shrill, flouncing Musetta

Colin Mason—THE DAILY TELEGRAPH March 3 1966

ANN HOWARD's great hoyden of a Musetta justified Marcello's description of her as a screech-owl (*civetta)* is used in two senses in the opera – though in the last act some tenderness did allay the acid of her tones.

Andrew Porter—THE FINANCIAL TIMES March 3 1966

ANN HOWARD, alas, was a shrill caricature of Musetta, got up like Santa Claus too.

Eric Mason—DAILY MAIL March 3 1966

By most standards, ANN HOWARD made a rather hoydenish Musetta, but it was a pleasure to hear the famous Waltz Song sung and not grimaced.

Richard Last—THE SUN March 3 1966

The choice of ANN HOWARD, a heavy-weight, muscular Musetta, no nymphomaniac firework, but a fearsome Ftatateeta, is clever, and justified against expectations.

Our Music Critic—THE TIMES March 3 1966

ANN HOWARD's brash Musetta is well contrasted to Mimi.

Leslie Ayre—EVENING NEWS March 3 1966

ANN HOWARD grotesquely overplayed Musetta (producer John Blachley to blame surely). The Wells has a high, middlebrow standard and ought to safeguard it more jealously.

Philip Hope-Wallace—THE GUARDIAN March 3 1966

A major part for Ann at this time was the Witch in Humperdinck's *Hansel and Gretel*. It was the first of the many roles that she describes as 'witches and bitches'.

The Gingerbread Witch in 'Hansel and Gretel' 1964
Photo: Donald Southern

Composers clearly feel that the mezzo soprano voice lends itself well to these colourful roles. There are very few evil roles for high sopranos – with exceptions like the Queen of the Night' in Mozart's *The Magic Flute.*

The part of the Witch had been sung many times by Sheila Rex, a singer a few years older than Ann. Ann took it over, but was embarrassed and saddened when she, rather than Sheila Rex, was chosen to make the television relay and the recording of the production. This was not to be the only example of the heartlessness of casting in the opera world.

PRESS

Hansel and Gretel by Engelbert Humperdinck Sadler's Wells 1965

Miss ANN HOWARD . . . one of the production's particular delights with her variety of subtle touches as the Witch

THE TIMES 1965

ANN HOWARD, the Witch . . . . bestrode the stage with a knowing leer and a voracious appetite.

Alan Blyth-THE DAILY EXPRESS 1965

ANN HOWARD'S vigorously projected Gingerbread Witch, slyly pantomimic and well sung..

A.E.P.—THE DAILY TELEGRAPH 1965

ANN HOWARD revelled in the part of the Witch; her portrayal was full of creative characterization.

Peter Holsworth

ANN HOWARD makes much of the beaky-nosed Witch and, while getting alal the fun out of the comical 'business' does not forget to sing forth substantially.

Leslie Ayre—EVENING NEWS

An intensely busy period of Ann's career now commenced. Her diary stated that she performed all over Britain, including Scotland; furthermore, as the principal singers often had roles in both the 'S' and the 'W' companies, it was not unusual to have to go back to London for a performance and then return to the touring city the next day.

Ann in the role of Jocasta in Stravinsky's opera 'Oedipus Rex' Photo: Reg Wilson

She remembers singing the part of Jocasta in Stravinsky's *Oedipus Rex* with a distinguished cast including Ronald Dowd, Alberto Remedios and Donald McIntyre, and on the same night singing a part in *L'heure Espangnole* by Ravel. She describes this as a 'divine piece' – very funny with much amusing stage business and a fabulous cast: Dennis Dowling David Bowman and Emile Belcourt. She also learned and performed the role of Ragonde in Rossini's opera *Count Ory*

Ann in the role of Ragonde in 'Count Ory' by Rossini in 1965
Photo: Donald Southern

PRESS

<u>Sadler's Wells productions of Oedipus Rex by Igor Stravinsky and L'Heure Espagnole by Maurice Ravel (a double bill) – in London and the Provinces</u>

ANN HOWARD, in a remarkable transformation from Jocasta in Stravinsky (Oedipus Rex) which she sang with a hardness of tone and distinct vibrato, to a quite luscious Conception in Ravel's horological comedy (L'Heure Espagnol) was the only singer to appear in both operas.

K.W. Dommett—BIRMINGHAM POST May 1967

. . . . Against these the ice-blue costume of Jocasta (ANN HOWARD) struck the same feminine contrast as her supple and shining soprano quality did as a foil to the timbre of the all male cast . . . . By contrast, the second item on the double bill, Ravel's ephemeral phantasy L'Heure Espagnol, flowed in one piece from the beginning to end. ANN HOWARD made a fetchingly beautiful and petulant Conception.

Horace Fitzpatrick—OXFORD MAIL May 24 1967

Oedipus . . . Ronald Dowd, ... was well matched by ANN HOWARD's impressive, almost too youthfully voluptuous Jocasta.

Ronald Crichton—THE FINANCIAL TIMES April 1967

ANN HOWARD acquitted herself nobly in Jocasta's long aria.

Stephen Walsh—OBSERVER April 2 1967

As the Sadlers Wells company performed in theatres that were considerably smaller than the Royal Opera House, they favoured operettas and The Savoy Operas of Gilbert and Sullivan. This suited Ann well as it was not such a big step from the West End musical stage which she still loved.

Ann as Queen of the Fairies in Gilbert and Sullivan's 'Iolanthe' with Stafford Dean as Private Willis

CHAPTER 6

An Expanding Operatic Career

1966.

'The Mines of Sulphur' 1966. Ann playing the part of Leda, one of the (ghostly) theatricals Photo: John Williams

Ann was now thirty-two. In February and March of this year she was regularly singing in *La bohème* (Musetta) for Sadlers Wells Opera, but was also expanding her work into doing concerts for the BBC. She was to work regularly for the BBC in the next years. An early BBC engagement took her to Jersey for a big opera concert. The very next day she was back doing *La bohème* again. She was also rehearsing Wagner's *Die Walküre* for Scottish Opera.

13th May saw the first night of *Die Walküre* in Glasgow, Ann singing the role of Fricka as well as one of the Valkyrie. (This was sung in German. She was later to be Fricka for English National Opera's famous English Ring Cycle under Reginald Goodall.) A number of further performances were sung in Edinburgh and Aberdeen.

A glance into her diary reveals an extraordinary few days in June of this year: June 7th singing the role of Fricka in Aberdeen; June 9th starting rehearsals for *The Mines of Sulphur* by Richard Rodney Bennett for

Sadler's Wells Opera in London ; June 10th back in Aberdeen for a further performance of *Die Walküre*. Such a schedule was not to be unusual from now on.

'The Mines of Sulphur' by Richard Rodney Bennett
1966 Photo: Zoe Dominic

The Mines of Sulphur was a major new work and this was to be the world première. It was conducted by Colin Davis and directed by Colin Graham. The story was about a group of theatricals (of whom Ann was one) who were in fact ghosts – having died of the plague. It was startling and horrific, though Ann remembers that there were wonderful comic moments too. The opera was a great success and was also made for television. The premiere performance in 1965 of this opera at the London Coliseum by Sadler's Wells Opera received universal praise for the musical direction, orchestral playing and the singing of the members of the cast under Colin Davis. The production of Colin Graham and the atmospheric staging of Alix Stone were also admired. However, there were mixed reviews for the music itself.

The opera received a revival in September 1973 and a television performance in November 1966.

PRESS

Revival of 'The Mines of Sulphur' by Richard Rodney Bennett. September 1973

Last night's revival at the London Coliseum (of 'The Mines of Sulphur), conducted by David Lloyd Jones, had much to recommend it – assured singing, fluent acting (including a *tour de force* performance from ANN HOWARD) and atmospheric staging.

Christopher Grier—EVENiNG STANDARD September 8 1973

ANN HOWARD stands out for the extravagance of her comic timing (Leda is a gift of a part)

Max Loppert—THE FINANCIAL TIMES September 28 1973

Like Britten , too (to whom the opera is dedicated) (Bennett) knows how to lighten the whole brooding atmosphere, making Madame Leda (ANN HOWARD), the magnificently upholstered prima donna of the troupe , into a comic figure of stature.

Hugo Cole—COUNTRY LIFE October 25 1973

Over the summer months of 1966 Ann's diary was full of rehearsals with Sadler's Wells Opera. One of her biggest and most important roles was in the making: ' Delilah' in Saint-Saëns's *Samson and Delilah*. The year ended with a busy December, singing the Witch in *Hansel and Gretel* and performances of *Oedipus Rex*.

Ann as Delilah in Saint-Saëns' opera 'Samson and Delilah' with Alberto Remedios as Samson 1966

I asked Ann to describe to me how she approached a major role like Delilah. What were her first thoughts, and how did she commence on the long journey to the first night? After only a few seconds of thought, and with a chuckle she said 'I find out how many arias there are'. What she discovered would alarm the bravest singer. It is a huge role with four major arias as well as extensive ensemble work, but she was undaunted. She read the text through and set about interpreting the character of Delilah and her relationships with the other characters. I asked her if she listened to recordings of the work to hear how other singers had sung the role. This, she assured me, she never does, preferring to have only her own ideas.

Act 3 of 'Samson and Delilah'

In describing Delilah, Ann said that there was no opportunity find a new personality for the role. Some roles – like that of Carmen – can be interpreted in many different ways and still stay faithful to the music and the plot. 'Delilah is a bitter and unpleasant person from the start', Ann assured me. 'Her only love is her pagan god Dagon, and all poetic descriptions and loving utterances are only a deceit.'

At Delilah's first entry, at the head of the Philistines' most seductive maidens, she sings a gentle aria remembering the love that she had given Samson when 'the sun laughed, the Spring awoke and kissed the ground'. Yet she is no gentle lover, but a cruel temptress. Samson is an enemy of her people and is the follower of a different god. Furthermore he left her after their earlier love-making and she harbours a potent hatred of him.

In the second act she is awaiting his arrival, summoning love to aid her in her mission to discover the secret of Samson's superhuman strength. She sings the second great aria 'Love, aid me in my cause.' The High Priest of Dagon exhorts her to use every means to exact revenge for the victory which Samson gained over the Philistines.

'Samson and Delilah': Act 2 'Softly awakes my heart' – Ann with Ronald Dowd

41

Samson appears, but instinctively knows that he should leave Delilah. However, she sings a wonderfully seductive aria – ' Softly Awakes My Heart ' – the most famous aria in the opera – and bewitches Samson. She learns the secret of his power: his hair. Delilah summons the Philistine soldiers and Samson is dragged away. He is blinded and his hair is cut. Samson is doomed – his strength completely lost. He is imprisoned and his people, the Hebrews, are overwhelmed by the Philistines.

The final scene includes a great aria for Delilah who is now all powerful. She mocks Samson mercilessly. The opera ends dramatically with Samson's sudden revival of strength and the destruction of the temple and all within it.

This rich plot makes for a perfect opera, and Saint-Saëns takes full advantage of the dramatic situations between the characters as well as giving a big role to the chorus. Ann told me that she had to know about each of the other roles and to work out exactly how she, as Delilah, would identify with them. She would need to express both her lust and her loathing of Samson and her religious fervour with the priest. In the first two acts she sings of love and the beauties of nature and employs every seductive trick to seduce Samson. In the last act she could give full rein to her triumph over Samson and allow her hatred to fully express itself.

She worked with repetiteurs for many months, spending a number of hours a week on the long task of learning and memorising the music. Bar-by-bar the role was built up. The music director also would rehearse with the principal singers to work on every aspect of the musical interpretation. Ann is quick to say that she was not a trained musician and needed to work with repetiteurs to learn a role. We discussed this and I suggested that, in a curious way, this was to her advantage. Singers who rely on their good music-reading skills often find memorising very difficult. She was able to memorise from the very beginning and would not experience the loss of the written music when production rehearsals began. During these early months she would also 'sing the role into the voice'. The vocal demands of the role of Delilah are very considerable. The music ranges over two octaves, often using the extremities of the voice to dramatic effect, and the role is very long. Furthermore, the arias become more and more demanding throughout the opera, so it is necessary to build up a lot of stamina.

With the music safely learned, production rehearsal start. I was surprised to learn that at that time only about three weeks were spent in production rehearsal. (Admittedly, it was not a new production, though of course it was new for Ann.) Towards the end of her career she worked on operas that had many more weeks for production, the whole emphasis then being almost more on the production than on the singing.

The first night of *Samson and Delilah* was on September 1st, 1966, in Coventry. Further performances were in Nottingham, Newcastle, Glasgow, Aberdeen, Edinburgh and Bradford. Unbelievably, during this tour, she was also rehearsing a role in Berlioz's *The Trojans* for a BBC Prom as well as a part in the Viennese operetta *Waltz Dream* by Oscar Straus, for the BBC. (Ann said that she always took every opportunity to sing operetta – she loved it so much.) The Samson and Delilah production moved to the Coliseum in London, opening on November 9th.

I asked Ann about her Samsons. This part was usually sung by Ronald Dowd, but sometimes by Ramon Remedios. She recounted a very sad story about a performance by Remedios. He had invited various guests and his agent to hear him and knew that his future career might depend on his performance. It got to the final scene when the temple collapses. Samson has some fine music to sing at this point, but somehow, because of a mix-up with various cues, the stage crew brought the scenery down far too early. This signalled a premature end to the opera and Remedios was unable to continue singing – a great disappointment for him.

PRESS

Sadler's Wells production of Saint-Saëns's opera 'Samson and Delilah' November 1968

. . . . musically, there was much to enjoy . . . . ANN HOWARD as Delilah could give several points to any recent Miss World in the matter of physical allure. She has a luscious voice too.

Noel Goodwin—DAILY EXPRESS November 16 1968

ANN HOWARD makes a queenly figure of Delilah. She sings the music with fine, firm-drawn lines . . . . a performance to admire.

Stanley Sadie—THE TIMES November 16 1968

. . . . for her nocturnal meeting with Samson, MISS HOWARD 's appearance in magnificent . . . . the voice becomes warmer . . . . more commanding than inviting . . . . She is at her best in the last act duet with the High Priest . . . . and here the Gorr-like firmness of MISS HOWARD's delivery is entirely right.

Ronald Crichton—THE FINANCIAL TIMES November 16 1968

ANN HOWARD's Delilah, firm of voice and figure . . . . this is a revival not to be missed.

Felix Aprahamian—SUNDAY TIMES November 17 1968

ANN HOWARD makes a first-rate Delilah. Her voice is full and clear, and she looks genuinely tempting even from the stalls . . .

Stephen Walsh—OBSERVER November 17 1968

ANN HOWARD, tall, beautiful and filling out the grand vocal line with ease and opulent variety of tone, was just the thing.

Philip Hope-Wallace—GUARDIAN November 16 1968

ANN HOWARD is surely the most eye-taking of all Delilahs, probably including the real one. But more than that, she is endowed with a dark smoky voice that admirably suits the role and she is an actress of intelligence.

Ernest Bradbury—YORKSHIRE POST April 9 1968

ANN HOWARD, a tall and voluptuous Delilah made a good deal of these arias: ' Softly Awakes' and 'Oh love from Thy Power' in last night's revival of the Sadler's Wells production conducted by Roderick Brydon

Eric Mason—DAILY MAIL November 16 1968

The two dominant characters are strongly cast. Any suggestion of 'ham' could easily make that second act laughable, but ANN HOWARD poises it very nicely and sings out in truly beguiling fashion.

Leslie Ayre—EVENING NEWS November 16 1968

ANN HOWARD looked regal and sang with a generous outpouring of tone..

Harold Rosenthal—OPERA January 1969

Last night in Theatre Royal, Newcastle (Samson and Delilah) looked and sounded better than ever. It would be difficult to imagine a more voluptuous, seductive, rich-voiced Delilah than ANN HOWARD, whose unforgettable performance of the exacting role brought the house down. Her famous aria 'Softly Awakes my Heart' was impressive.

John Healey—THE JOURNAL, NEWCASTLE February 26 1969

ANN HOWARD was a tall, comely Delilah, not in the least absurd as that voluptuary often appears in minor revivals of the work . . . . Her voice sounded rich, warm, dark . . . . this was no mere oratorio hooting.

P.H.W.—OPERA January 1967

Fortunately the Wells have a team of voices which . . . manages . . . to approach the heroic scale of Keith Beattie's production and Ralph Koltai's sets. ANN HOWARD . . . . is still an effective Delilah. And if she evokes Ruben's rather than Hollywood's picture of the temptress, this matches the richness and sheer technical assurance of her voice.

J.C.—THE SCOTSMAN September 23 1966

ANN HOWARD, Scottish Opera's Fricka, made a strong and impressive Delilah, and could cope (as her predecessor here could not) with both the top notes and the bottom notes of her part.

Conrad Wilson—THE SCOTSMAN October 7 1966

Ann's first appearance as Delilah in November 1966

Miss Howard is a handsome and seductive Delilah, and she sustained her long scene with some well-shaped and expressively alive singing in which an occasional want of volume was a small price to pay for the absence of all plumminess of tone and enunciation.

Colin Mason—THE TELEGRAPH November 10 1966

Urged by a most competent orchestra under the baton of John Barker, the artists gave a dazzling performance (making) the singing and acting of ANN HOWARD as Delilah and Alberto Remedios as Samson memorable.

A.J.M.

ANN HOWARD is an incisive singer with some ugly timbres in her voice, and a lack of sensuous intensity in her delivery; striking in appearance, Artemis rather than Aphrodite, her Delilah looks best in statuesque poses – her movements are often stiff and uncomfortable.

Our Music Critic—THE TIMES November 10 1966

ANN HOWARD ,the Delilah, proved voluptuous of voice and presence, and through her consummate acting, established the love-hate complex between these two participants (Samson and Delilah).

M.C.—YORKSHIRE POST

It would be difficult to find two principals more completely suited in voice and appearance than Alberto Remedios and ANN HOWARD who played the title roles. Miss Howard's rich, even-toned quality of voice gave immense pleasure and Mr Remedios matched it with splendidly ringing resonant tone.

John Healy

Ronald Dowd and ANN HOWARD both new to their roles in the Sadler's Wells revival on November 9 (1066) did much to bring their characters to life by spirited attack and sustained intensity.

THE STAGE November 1966

Tall and rich in the requisite allure, MISS HOWARD brings off her big scene ("Softly awakes my heart") securely and convincingly. The middle of her voice sometimes fades in volume, but she always sings stylishly.

Leslie Ayre—EVENING NEWS November 10 1966

ANN HOWARD and Ronald Dowd offer splendidly full-bodied assumptions of the rewarding parts of heroine and hero, only wanting a little more flow and legato. When things have settled down more under James Matheson's baton, the result could hold up its head anywhere from Brussels to Bordeaux.

Philip Hope-Wallace—GUARDIAN November 10 1966

ANN HOWARD the Well's statuesque mezzo-soprano was perhaps the most convincing Delilah, vocally and physically, I have heard.

Richard last—THE SUN November 11 1966

ANN HOWARD, the tall new Delilah, was agreeably warm-toned and looked enticing enough to seduce a whole host of Israelites. Deliciously voluptuous in 'Softly Awakes' she hadn't quite the strength to project the lowest notes of 'O Love from thy Power'.

Eric Mason—DAILY MAIL November 10 1966

The cast is dominated visually by ANN HOWARD's majestic, magnificently beautiful Delilah . . . . Ann Howard, as I have suggested, is so glorious to look at that I can hardly trust myself to criticise her singing impartially. Throughout her first scene I was, however, bothered by the conviction that there must be a larger, more commanding voice there than she was producing. As the evening went on she grew in vocal confidence. She does not yet project a full ample line in the part. But vocally it is a promising, and by no means unpleasing performance.

David Cairns—THE FINANCIAL TIMES November 10 1966

1967.

The year began with many performances of *Hansel and Gretel, Oedipus Rex, L'heure Espagnole, Iolanthe* and *Samson and Delilah.* Her role in *Iolanthe* was the Fairy Queen which has a very low tessitura. The famous aria 'O Foolish Fey' was transposed up for her. There were also regular engagements and recordings for the BBC. These were most often programmes of light music like *Grand Hotel, Vienna, City Of Dreams* or radio performances of operettas such as *The Arcadians.* Ann genuinely loved this music and said that she could have made her whole career with it. She recorded *The Dancing Years* for EMI. Ann also joined two of her colleagues, Mary Illing and David Winnard, for concert-party performances up and down the country. For these engagements, which were not part of her contract with an opera company, she had to find her own repetiteur.

In August she started rehearsing Stravinsky's *The Rake's Progress* in which Ann played Baba the Turk. Her diary was full to the end of the year.

1968

Two important things happened at the start of this year: she began work on *Ariadne auf Naxos* by Richard Strauss and she found that she was expecting a baby.

Ann as the Composer in 'Ariadne auf Naxos' by Richard Strauss   Photo: Donald Southern

Ariadne, she told me, was extremely difficult and had a high tessitura. She was still singing the Witch in *Hansel and Gretel*, and doing engagements with the BBC while rehearsing *Ariadne* – and popping off to have check-ups at the ante-natal clinic. The first night of was on March 15th, performed for Youth And Music. Other performances followed but Ann was not entirely happy with the role. She found the range very high and unsuitable for her voice. She got good reviews for her performance, but she decided not to sing it again even when she was invited to do it later in Canada. It takes a certain sort of courage to turn down major roles in this competitive industry, but voices can be damaged, or even ruined, by singing unsuitable or stressful music.

Ann's pregnancy in no way interfered with her busy schedule. She was doing regular performances of *Ariadne* and rehearsing with the BBC for a radio performance of Dvořák's *Rusalka* conducted by Vilem Tausky in which she played the Witch. Somehow she also fitted in a number of concerts. These were opera evenings of arias from many different operas. She especially remembers concerts in Wales which she found very demanding as her enthusiastic audience always wanted encores at the end of a taxing performance.

She was singing the role of the Fairy Queen in Gilbert and Sullivan's *Iolanthe*. In this production she had to be raised up off the stage in a fairy's grand chair. Keith was alarmed that his pregnant wife should endanger herself with wobbly scenery, but happily there were no mishaps. A month before the birth Ann was in a recording of Lionel Monckton's *The Arcadians* for EMI with June Bronhill and David Hughes.

The season ended in June. On August 21st Ann and Keith welcomed their baby daughter into the world and named her Katherine Jane Elizabeth.

A long maternity leave was not planned for Ann. By October she was doing a concert in Scarborough and starting rehearsals for *Samson and Delilah* for Sadlers Wells Opera. She was also soon back on the road, touring with the company. In November Samson and Delilah opened at the Coliseum.

Peering into her 1968 diary she was astonished to see that after the first night of *Samson and Delilah*, on the day of the second performance, she was working with the BBC on the opera *Cendrillon* by Massenet. This entailed a 2.30pm – 5.30pm rehearsal before going on stage as Delilah in the evening. This happened on several subsequent days before the eventual recording of *Cendrillon* for the BBC took place over an entire Saturday. How could she – and her voice – cope with such a schedule? Perhaps the answer is because she really loved what she was doing and enjoyed every moment. She was also gifted with excellent health and an equally healthy voice production. However, few singers would take on so much, especially only three months after giving birth. Performances of *Samson and Delilah* continued, and she fitted in *Grand Hotel* for the BBC, a live programme that went out on a Sunday evening; Ann sang popular arias and ballads.

As the run of performances ended in December ,Ann was beginning to work on a truly mammoth project with Sadler's Wells Opera: Wagner's *Ring* conducted by Reginald Goodall. For the first time this epic work was going receive a performance in English, and was later always referred to as 'The English Ring'. *The Valkyrie* was the first of the four operas to be produced. Ann had already performed this with Scottish Opera, singing in German. Now she had to learn her role as Fricka in English, and to be rehearsed in painstaking detail by Goodall.

Ann in the role of Fricka in Wagner's opera 'The Valkyrie' Photo: Anthony Crickmay

1969.

Ann has fond memories of the early rehearsals with Goodall which commenced on January 6th. They were held in his eyrie in the upper amphitheatre at Covent Garden – a tiny room. ('Like a lavatory' according to Ann.) She remembers how each bar would be worked at very thoroughly, (and there are a lot of bars); perhaps 20 minutes would be spent on a couple of phrases.

She loved working with this man who had such a passion for the music and who was able to inspire great enthusiasm in everyone involved. It is extremely unusual for the musical director to rehearse with the singers at this early stage. Singers would normally work with repetiteurs, only working with the musical director once the work was committed to memory.

Ann was delighted to be rehearsed by Goodall. He had very definite ideas about tempi and phrasing which she learned from the very start. By the time the production rehearsals began every singer was totally familiar with the conductor's requirements. This was the first important ingredient in what became an enormous success

PRESS

Die Walkure by Richard Wagner. Ann first sang the role of Fricka for Scottish Opera (in German) in 1966. The production toured to Aberdeen

Scottish Opera began its visit to Aberdeen with a superb performance of Die Walkure in His Majesty's theatre last night . . . . The chief of the gods, as portrayed by Herbert Hofmann, was a tragic figure – all powerful, but so weary of it. His wife, Fricka, was beautifully sung by ANN HOWARD, who seemed much too nice a lady to be demanding Siegmund's death.

D.l.W.—SCOTTISH EVENING NEWS 1966

THE VALKYRIE New production at the London Coliseum: Sadler's Wells Opera

Entitled: 'The Valkyries ride into triumph – in plain English'

A foretaste of Wagner's cycle of 'Ring' operas in English, before they return to the English National Opera repertory next month, is far and away the best pre-Christmas item at the Coliseum.

These performances of 'The Valkyrie' alone are conducted by Reginald Goodall, and will form the basis of a later gramophone album. His superb shaping of the music is sustained by orchestral playing of warmth and grandeur, and also of heartfelt intensity and delicacy. It exposes the fallacy that singers in Wagner have to bawl to be heard, and makes it possible to follow almost every detail in the excellent English version.

I have seldom heard the love scene of Siegmund and Sieglinde more tenderly sung than between Alberto Remedios, now in specially fine voice, and Margaret Curphy. The same goes for the eloquent dialogue of Brunnhilde and Wotan, and their majestic closing scene . . . . . with ANN HOWARD's imperious Fricka, a jolly group of helmeted Valkyries and the general excellent stage representation, the long evening (five hours) is continuously absorbing.

Noel Goodwin

ANN HOWARD's Fricka is likewise younger than this role is usually presented. And again it makes sense. She is the boss's wife: sophisticated, handsome, self-assertive, and above all determined that neither his mistaken decision nor his extra-marital affairs are going to undermine her position. Here is no nagging Hausfrau but an executive who thinks she knows better and has no qualms about interfering. Her direct if unsubtle singing supported this conception of the role.

Bryan Magee—MUSIC AND MUSICIANS March 1970

Amid the black and silver moondust and meteorites of the Act 2 set, NORMAN BAILEY's shifty yet sympathetic Wotan and ANN HOWARD's imperious Fricka were strongly presented.

Noel Goodwin DAILY EXPRESS January 31 1970

. . . . exceptionally sensitive to the test, as was ANN HOWARD in her splendid characterisation of Fricka, perfectly conveying the mixture of sarcasm and indignation in her tirade at Wotan.

Colin Mason—DAILY TELEGRAPH January 31 1970

. . . . ANN HOWARD, an alarmingly vehement Fricka

John Warrack—THE SUNDAY TIMES February 1 1970

. . . . Because the distinguished team responsible have made certain that so much can be seen, heard and understood, it is powerful theatrical as well as musical experience . . . . . ANN HOWARD's Fricka is a formidable, handsome creature, scoring her points with such sadistic glee that one feels more than usually sorry for Wotan.

Ronald Crichton—FINANCIAL TIMES January 31 1970

. . . for me, was one of the great evenings in the opera house. It was so satisfying aesthetically and dramatically . . . . I have never been so intellectually satisfied as on this occasion . . . . ANN HOWARD's voice is more soprano than mezzo, and I like my Fricka to sing in rich rounded tones; but MISS HOWARD's singing was so purposeful and clear, and her conception of the role so vivid, that i was prepared to forgive her everything else. She knew how to plead Fricka's cause in more senses than one.

Harold Rosenthall—OPERA March 1970

I happen to like ANN HOWARD's sometimes coldly instrumental, not to say inhuman, tones as Fricka. After all, she was surely just this kind of martinet god-wife to Wotan. There is room for a difference of opinion here, although I fear it might be true that too much Wagnerian singing on this scale would knock all the tenderness out of a voice still obviously capable of tenderness. It is, nevertheless, a compelling performance. Stewart Deas—COUNTRY LIFE August 16 1973

<u>Reviews of a performance of 'The Valkyrie' at Manchester Opera House 1975</u>

It is a pity that no curtain calls are being taken after each act (why not?) for the audience – again filling the theatre to suffocation – would have liked to acclaim the truly fine singing of ANN HOWARD as Fricka in Act 11, a strong and vivid performance of this horrid sample of outraged marital virtue.

Michael Kennedy—THE DAILY TELEGRAPH June 5 1975

In general, it is a very competent cast, with ANN HOWARD's Fricka and Derek Hammond Stroud's Alberich outstandingly better than that.

Gerald Larner—THE GUARDIAN June 3 1975

ANN HOWARD's Act 11 singing of Fricka was another of the many good things. It was a superb performance, and so was that of Harold Blackburn as a resonant and refined Hunding.

John Robert-Blunn—MANCHESTER EVENING NEWS June 4 1975

Of course, Sadler's Wells Opera was revelling in its new, and far bigger home at the London Coliseum. It was also right in the middle of London's theatre-land, giving it a far higher profile than in their days in Islington. It also invited larger productions than were possible in the old theatre. The 'Ring' was an obvious choice – though to do it in English was somewhat controversial.

Other large-scale operas were produced – of course in English: Richard Strauss's *Der Rosencavalier* and Verdi's *Don Carlos* and a whole sequence of ambitious modern operas; but it was the *Ring* which was the most significant. The company produced each of the four operas over the following years, eventually being able to run them all in sequence over a period of a week.

In 1974 the cumbersome title of 'Sadler's Wells Opera at the London Coliseum' was eventually changed to 'English National Opera'. ENO , England's first national opera that would always perform in English (with the one exception of Stravinsky's *Oedipus Rex* which was sung in Latin).

People loved it. The creation of this company did much to gain a far bigger audience for opera than had been known in Britain before. To this day it maintains an egalitarian atmosphere, denying opera the elite profile that it has at Covent Garden or Glyndebourne. Scottish Opera and Welsh National Opera, and eventually English Opera North were to follow.

1969

Ann as Proserpina in 'L'Orfeo' by Monteverdi Photo: Houston Rogers

Towards the end of January, with *The Valkyrie* still in rehearsal, Ann again worked for the BBC on a production of *The Mock Doctor* – (a rare work by Gounod) in Manchester and was the cover for the role of Cassandra in *The Trojans* at Covent Garden (in French). She was also rehearsing two parts in Monteverdi's *Orfeo* for ENO. This opened on March 20th, conducted by Raymond Leppard with John Wakefield as Orfeo. Unbelievably, her diary also discloses that she was doing intermittent performances of *Samson and Delilah* in Newcastle.

As the season progressed Ann was rehearsing Berlioz's *The Trojans* for Scottish Opera (in English). This was a massive work – in fact two operas: *The Trojans at Carthage* and *The Fall of Troy*, collectively lasting over seven hours in performance. Ann had the role of Cassandra which is in the first of these. She wryly remembers that she had to wait a number of hours during the second opera to sing just one line – 'They will build Troy anew' – from behind a stage curtain! She also remembers sharing a dressing room with Janet Baker.

A scene from Scottish Opera's production of 'The Trojans' by Berlioz: Ann playing Cassandra Photo: Bryan and shear Ltd

The first night was on May 3rd in Glasgow; performances followed in Edinburgh, Aberdeen and Newcastle. In an astonishing week in June, Ann was working every day on three different projects: with the BBC (*Mavra* by Stravinsky and *Ulysses* by Dallapiccola); with Covent Garden ('*The Trojans* in which she covered the role of Cassandra – now in French – and for which she was fully rehearsed) and again with the BBC at the Royal Festival Hall for *Grand Hotel*. She confesses that she has no memory of this, but her diary bears witness to it.

One thing she remembers vividly was an occasion at the Royal Opera when the German singer who was playing Cassandra failed to appear until the very last moment. Meanwhile, Ann had put on the costume and was fully made up and ready to go on stage. With less than an hour to the start of the performance, the singer rushed into the theatre and Ann had to bear the disappointment of not singing that night.

A period of intense learning work followed with daily sessions with repetiteurs for *The Rake's Progress* by Stravinsky for ENO – Ann to play Baba the Turk ('I loved it' she said) and comic role of Boulotte in Offenbach's opera *Bluebeard*.

Ann as Baba the Turk in Stravinsky's opera 'The Rake's Progress'
Photo: Donald Southern

In the new season this busy schedule continued. *The Trojans* at Covent Garden opened on September 17th (Ann covering Cassandra). *Valkyrie* was still in rehearsal for ENO and there were intermittent dates with the BBC. Performances of *The Rake's Progress' and Bluebeard* commenced and a tour to Northern cities and Scotland followed.

1970

The Valkyrie opened on January 29th after over a year in rehearsal. It caused a sensation in the opera world. Opinions on the merits and demerits of performing Wagner in any other language than German filled the arts columns of the press, but the success of the production was immediate. Reginald Goodall became a household name and new star singers were born, notably Rita Hunter, Alberto Remedios and Norman Bailey. Ann had the role of Fricka and was part of the overall success. Performances continued through January and February.

PRESS

Ariadne auf Naxos by Richard Strauss and The Rake's Progress by Igor Stravinsky

Sadler's Well Opera production of 'Ariadne auf Naxos' by Richard Strauss. March 1968

ANN HOWARD (as 'The Composer') makes a tall and strikingly handsome boy, more young Strauss than young Mozart. Her features radiate sincerity. The sudden infatuation for Zerbinetta was charmingly conveyed. Her singing was and forthright . . .

Ronald Crichton—THE FINANCIAL TIMES March 20 1968

Review of the same performance

The composer was sung for the first time by ANN HOWARD. Attractive in appearance, sympathetic in manner and basically with the right quality of voice. The lower range of the music fared best from her last night.

Joan Chissell—THE TIMES March 20 1968

Sadler's Wells Opera production of 'The Rake's Progress' by Stravinsky November 1969

. . . a superb study of Baba from ANN HOWARD D.F.B. THE STAGE November 1969

. . . an outstanding Baba from ANN HOWARD, who splendidly overcame the notorious difficulties of making this part effective.

Colin Mason—THE TELEGRAPH November 21 1969

The versatile ANN HOWARD is effective in the role of Baba, the Turk, the bearded lady . . . . She actually makes this strange character almost credible.

Leslie Ayre EVENING NEWS November 21 1969

Baba – the superb ANN HOWARD

Stephen Walsh THE OBSERVER November 23 1969

ANN HOWARD a highly effective Baba

SUNDAY TIMES November 23 1969

ANN HOWARD'S loquaciously domineering

Eric Mason DAILY MAIL November 23 1969

. . . for Baba, ANN HOWARD was an uncommonly winning bearded beauty, with a welcome twinkle in the eye.

Joan chisell THE TIMES November 23 1969

ANN HOWARD'S performance as Baba the Turk was delightful. She has a splendid voice and, while she revelled in the opportunities which the character offered, she never at any time overplayed it.

T.W. THE SCOTSMAN November 1969

ANN HOWARD is the best Baba I have heard – and she looks truly magnificent.

Harold Rosenthall OPERA January 1970

CHAPTER 7

Carmen And An International Career

Ann had played the comic and sexy role of Boulotte in Offenbach's *Bluebeard* for ENO. A producer that saw her in this realised that she could be a Carmen. This popular Bizet opera was already in the ENO repertory, but a new production was planned to be produced by John Copley. Ann was thrilled and excited to be asked to take on the role. She remembers breaking the news to Keith with great delight. It was to be a turning point in her career.

Carmen Photo: Donald Southern

She had just two months to learn and rehearse the role. I asked how she set about it. She spoke in detail of the personality of Carmen and how she responded to every phrase.

There are as many interpretations of the role of Carmen as there are singers who perform it. Ann instinctively saw her as a spirited, fun-loving girl; a flirt who knew she could attract men but who was in no way a 'femme fatale'. Yes, she was sexy, but not a girl who would (in Ann's words) 'wrap her legs around the stage furniture in an overtly sexual way'. She was selfish and perhaps rather shallow, but was capable of falling in love in a romantic way.

Ann discussed all of her ideas with John Copley, and they seldom disagreed. Copley took an intense interest in every aspect of the opera, even to detailed discussions on costumes and wigs. Ann felt that, in many ways, the production was being built around her, and this she greatly appreciated. So much of her work in opera had been singing as a member of a team – one of the cast. Now she was the central figure, and on her portrayal lay the success of the production.

She was helped a great deal by James Craig, the repetiteur. Carmen's part is very long and there was a great deal to memorise in quite a short period of time. Craig made sure that she knew it all by greeting her at the beginning of each session with a portion of her music. He would play an extract from any part of the opera, even from the middle of an aria or ensemble, and expect her to immediately pick it up. This worked well, and in production she was able to confidently sing the music and concentrate on acting the part.

Craig's wife, Constance (Connie) also worked for the company as a production assistant. She knew the opera as well as the singers. Ann recounted the amazing story that, on a dress rehearsal, David Hughes, who sang the role of Don José, became ill, and Connie quickly stepped in and sang and acted the role – confidently hugging Carmen when required as she knew all the moves. Ann was astonished and delighted.

The opera opened on May 6th 1970 to ecstatic reviews. It was a triumph for John Copley, ENO and, of course, Ann. As the run started – and there were two performances a week right through the summer

– influential people from all over the world came to see it. For Ann, a series of connections pointed her towards the next stage of her career.

PRESS

Reviews of the first night of *Carmen* by Georges Bizet May 7 1970

Carmen reads the cards: 'Death!' Photo: Donald Southern

. . . . a real character, beautiful, confident and menacing, superior but isolated by her gipsy blood and hence contemptuous of, but very much part of, her surroundings . . . . . warm and responsive; she sings musically and with a sharp relish of the sensuous lines.

John Warrack—THE SUNDAY TELEGRAPH 10 May 1970

Ann as Carmen with David Hughes (Don José) Photo: Donald Southern

. . . . has an unusual ability to convey a wilful strength of character that is quite as essential to the role as the conventional sexual exuberance . . . . . an arresting performance . . . . Miss Howard's ability to project character.

Peter Heyworth THE OBSERVER 10 May 1970

Carmen in Act 3

Magnetic Carmen . . . . real fascination in the person of Carmen . . . . the hub of the matter. If you can't believe in the seductive magnetism of the Carmen, the opera collapses – yes, even if she can sing. ANN HOWARD, last seen as the majestic guardian of marriage in 'The Valkyrie', makes a tall, graceful, wholly self-possessed femme fatale; she struck precisely the right note in act 2, for instance, as she leant against a ladder on one side of the stage watching Escamillo – one graceful animal following with cool interest, no more, the doings of another . . . .. her Chanson Boheme had real dash and brilliance, and her final scene carried complete conviction.

Desmond Shaw-Taylor—THE SUNDAY TIMES 10 May 1970

Ann with Plácido Domingo in Guadalajara

In many ways this is the most vivid presentation of the opera I have ever seen . . . . . not there (London), nor in Naples, New York, Chicago or Bremen, nowhere have I encountered a Carmen which seemed to me to realise so vividly what Bizet intended by each passage as does the new Sadler's Wells production that opened on Wednesday . . . . . In ANN HOWARD'S heroine there are no affectations, no traditional seduction-routines. She makes a very attractive Carmen, voluptuous, fearless, honest by her lights: a complete and believable character. Her singing is strong and accomplished . . . . the expression is always right. She moves well, with both dignity and allure in her supple bearing.

Andrew Porter—THE FINANCIAL TIMES 7/8 May 1970

Three ENO Carmens: Ann, Katherine Pring and Gillian Knight

Sadler's Well Opera recently fielded as ideal a Carmen as any national company could wish . . . . For this new production by John Copley a quite different cast was assembled . . . . . ANN HOWARD promised badly for the role of all roles which demands total sexual appeal. Wonder of wonders. She has turned herself into a magnetic, interesting, subtle Carmen, adding flexibility of physical movement and instant allure to that dignity which we have admired in her work before . . . . . her attack in the Seguidilla and the card trio and the final duet is riveting: she leaves no doubt that Carmen is the most marvellous female role in all opera, and that she knows this, and will bring more and more to it.

William Mann – THE TIMES May 7 1970

Ann with 'Carmen' colleagues (l) David Hughes (Don José) and (r) Geoffrey Chard (Escamillo)

Thankfully, the new Carmen at the Coliseum is not one of those gypsy girls with a wicked laugh, shaking hips and all smouldering provocation. The time has surely arrived for Carmen to play cool and this ANN HOWARD does successfully . . . . . MISS HOWARD is a handsome girl and in her cool way can be just as seductive as the more conventional femme fatale. She is a thoughtful Carmen aware of her beauty and attractions for men and she rose powerfully to the dramatic scene at the end with Don Jose . . . . . bewitchingly attractive. Her Habanera was memorable. MISS HOWARD is the principal adornment of this new production which looks lavish and has plenty of action.

Sydney Edwards—EVENING STANDARD May 7 1970

The singing has a commanding focus in the Carmen of ANN HOWARD—tall and seductively glamorous, with a voice of wide musical expression and keen character.

Noel Goodwin—DAILY EXPRESS May 7 1970

. . . . Carmen is shown as the only person who can set this place alight, and she does so almost at once . . . . Much of the sexuality comes from the shape and person of ANN HOWARD . . . . as Carmen. For two or three minutes ANN HOWARD, black hair flowing over her shoulders, poses on a ladder, for all the world like Rita Heyworth in her cover girl period, simply challenging Jose to ignore her . . . . The voice is warm and agile, getting round both Habanera and sequidilla easily and cutting across the house without using a great deal of volume . . . . And that last act cought the power and excitement provided by Carmen herself . . . . she is no longer the tart but the grande dame, elegant in her white finery . . . . Don Jose's dagger kills, not a slut, but someone quite close to looking like a lady.

John Higgins—THE SPECTATOR MAY 16 1970

. . . . Indeed, in so many performances of the piece, the Carmen is so ludicrous that the audience's interest is switched to the decline and fall of Don Jose. Here, thanks to ANN HOWARD, the balance is restored. Hers is a Carmen for our times: a great big sexy girl, down to earth, utterly realistic, revelling in her own sensuality and enjoying life to the last drop . . . . And ANN HOWARD can sing too, as admirers of her Delilah and Fricka will recall.

Bill Croft—WHAT'S ON IN LONDON May 15 1970

John Copley, producer of this excellent new production (of Carmen) for Sadler's Wells Opera, is lucky to have an ideal Carmen to hand in ANN HOWARD. Between them they get miles away from the standard old operatic femme fatale and create a credible, hot-blooded woman whose behaviour is so consistent and logical that Jose's demands on her seem as outrageous to the audience as they do to her. ANN HOWARD'S is the most sympathetic, complete (and sexy) Carmen I have seen and she sings it better than most.

Rodney Milnes—QUEEN early June 1970

Carmen, in the shape of ANN HOWARD, is not your usual smouldering voluptuary, but a fearless, earthy, alluring gipsy quite out of the run of the normal interpreter. And her sense of fun in taunting the dragoons, and one dragoon in particular, helps to establish a rounded character. As I have already suggested, ANN HOWARD was dramatically an interesting Carmen . . . . she rose to the melodrama of the denouement, haughtily scorning Jose's advances in tone and demeanour.

Alan Blyth—OPERA July 1970

1st revival of the new production at the London Coliseum AUGUST 1970

No wonder WINTON DEAN, our leading Bizet scholar, has roundly declared that this is the best London revival of the work in the past 40 years . . . . ANN HOWARD's much-praised Carmen goes from strength to strength. Her long-limbed allure set off by the right element of hauteur is surely just what Merimee and Bizet had in mind, and her singing last night seemed to have won a new freedom and intensity – the card scene in particular. This interpretation would go anywhere in the world but it does particularly well at the Coliseum because Miss Howard knows, as few British singers know, how to match English words to music and, of course how to hold her audience, and her stage admirers, in the palm of her hands – hands that are pretty smart at a touch of karate if anyone gets too close to her . . . . has done nothing better in this house.

Alan Blyth—THE TIMES August 5 1970

. . . . the best London revival of the opera in the last 40 years. ANN HOWARD's Carmen was well sung and conspicuously well acted, rich in sexual allure but not crudely animal; the capacity for emotion she showed in Act 2 (she does love Jose, if not for long) strengthened the impact of the whole opera . . . . . The shade of Bizet, grievously wronged in recent years, must be resting appeased.

Winton Dean—THE MUSICAL TIMES July 1970

There has been a sort of glamour barrier which this production confidently sweeps aside . . . . . Glamour too in much of the singing, notably in ANN HOWARD's 'Carmen' , warm-voiced and seductive, a woman with far more than a snarl and a rose between her teeth, beautiful to look at and . . . . beautiful to hear.

Edward Greenfield—THE GUARDIAN August 5 1970

The new season of opera at the Coliseum opened with a performance of Bizet's Carmen, in which the title role was done great visual and vocal justice by ANN HOWARD. It was a captivating performance.

Michael Reynolds—DAILY MAIL August 5 1970

. . . . But John Copley makes ANN HOWARD a much deeper character; in tiny details, like Carmen being finally trapped by Don Jose because she trips over the fine white gown she is not yet used to wearing; and in the dignity and womanly compassion which makes her face the encounter instead of heeding the warning, and which disarms her fear until the last moment. These points I risk repeating because I saw the production for the first time last night, and therefore noticed them the more strongly. And the atmosphere, particularly in Past's smokey tavern, deserves repeated praise in any case.

Gillian Widdicombe—THE FINANCIAL TIMES August 5 1970

. . . . It is hard to imagine a better start than Bizet's brilliantly colourful and tune-packed masterpiece, of which the lavish Sadler's Wells production conducted by Charles Mackerras gives a very good idea. Carmen herself is, of course, at the centre of it and ANN HOWARD's portrayal of the gipsy girl is completely credible. She sings the role securely and, though one accepts her as one of the crowd of cigarette girls, there is a difference about her. She is forthright but yet retains an air of mystery – just the sort of girl a shy young dragoon might fall for.

Leslie Ayre—EVENING NEWS August 5 1970

I had missed the earlier performances, and despite the enthusiasm displayed by virtually all my colleagues, I was not wildly excited by the prospect of a long evening of Carmen on one of the summer's hottest and most humid of nights. Truth to tell, I had, until this evening fallen out of love with Carmen; I had begun to find it a bit of a bore, and rather less of a masterpiece that its advocates have long claimed it to be . . . . . But after this highly enjoyable and convincing performance, my faith in, and admiration for Carmen were restored.

The success of this production is the result of the excellent fusion of the musical and dramatic sides of the work into a convincing whole, aided by ANN HOWARD's outstanding performance in the title role. In other words, Sadler's Wells has achieved first-rate music theatre. And even if Carmen is an opera-comique with spoken dialogue, it fits naturally into the large stage and auditorium of the Coliseum.

ANN HOWARD, surely the most striking looking British female opera singer on the stage today, is a handsome, aristocratic and musical Carmen. How well she moves, and how pointedly she delivers the English text – the excellent John and Nell Moody version. Following so soon on her outstanding Fricka, (Die Walkure) I feel sure that MISS HOWARD is now well on the way to becoming a mature and full artist, and one with a very exciting future.

Harold Rosenthal—OPERA September 1970

Entitled: A TRIUMPHANT CARMEN The new season at the Coliseum opened on August 4th with a revival of Carmen, one of the best performances seen in London for years. ANN HOWARD's interpretationa of the title role was a personal triumph, as convincing a character portrayal as anyone could wish to see. This gipsy girl was a social misfit in urban society, indulging in the passions abut never allowing herself to be dominated by them. Carmen has many different facets. In Act 1 she is wayward, in Act 2 fascinated by a handsome soldier, in Act 3 reconciled to her fate, in the fourth act she goes, full of pride and anguish, to her death. HOWARD brought out all these elements in Carmen's character. Her singing was intelligent and well phrased. In the last act her transformation in appearance was a little radical, but this in no way detracted from the excellence of the overall interpretation.

John Greenhalgh—MUSIC AND MUSICIANS October 1970

Press reviews of subsequent performances of Carmen

King's theatre, Edinburgh 1972

In ANN HOWARD'S Carmen of course, it has a star – for a production of Carmen is nothing if it does not boast an outstanding exponent of the title role . . . . . MISS HOWARD makes a bold and thrilling Carmen: sexy but not a slut: honest, humorous, poised and beautiful, vocally admirable.

Conrad Wilson—SCOTSMAN—April 27 1972

The tall and shapely Carmen of ANN HOWARD gives a fiery focus to this most popular of operas, vividly staged to open a new season by the Sadler's Wells company.

Miss Howard not only looks both luscious and dangerous, but sings with a feeling for Bizet's familiar music which gives it fresh impact.

Noel Goodwin—DAILY EXPRESS July 31 1972

ANN HOWARD's Carmen certainly has sex. She has the kind of voice that goes with Sofia Loren, with accessories to match. Eyes flash, limbs move sinuously. It is a fiery display that sets sparks to the whole evening. But tender feelings as well as passion smoulder under the witchery aand in the card scene – almost Wagnerian – and the tragic end you are aware that there is something more than gipsy in her soul.

Ivon Adams—EVENING NEWS July 31 1972

Mr (Nicholas) Braithwaite's serious, sometimes heroic view of the score was well seconded by ANN HOWARD'a no-nonsense Carmen, which, once again, matched long-limbed allure with an element of dignity; this Gypsy is no slut. Miss Howard develops the character nicely from the carefree charmer of the first act through the bored fatalist of act three to the tragic figure of the finale.

Alan Blyth—THE TIMES JULY 31 1972

Ascending to the auditorium for Act 2, it was encouraging to find how well the orchestra were playing under Nicholas Braithwaite, and that ANN HOWARD was as impressive a Carmen as she had sounded below stairs. Her voice has both quality and power, and she manages to be both passionate and masterful quite without theatrical flaunting. In physique, movements and use of facial expression, she suggests one of Shaw's bold, wilful English heroines rather than a Spanish gipsy; but she is forceful and vivid in a way that makes Jose's infatuated helplessness believable (when we find a Jose ineffectual, aren't we usually criticising the Carmen of the evening for failing to provide adequate motivation?)

Hugo Cole—THE GUARDIAN July 31 1972

Press reviews of the 1974 revival of Carmen at The London Coliseum

Howard was in fine voice on the first night if this mid-revival cast change, and her highly individual interpretation was as intriguing as ever. The single most remarkable facet of her performance is its total lack of self-consciousness; no operatic hip-swinging, no Hollywood false allure – her, simply is an uncomplicated, very attractive girl who knows quite well to what use she can put the special talents the good Lord has given her, and would surely have died in her bed had she not had the misfortune to get fleetingly entangled with a dangerously unbalanced tenor. The air of sweet reason with which she starts the final duet is especially convincing. Her performance throws interesting light on the opera, and in particular on the difference between Bizet's Carmen and the murderous gipsy of Merimee's masterly novella. Music as passionate as this sweeps away the detachment of the original: you have to take sides. And with a Carmen as honest and reasonable as Miss Howard's there is little doubt as to whose case seems the most persuasive.

Rodney Milnes—OPERA May 1974

. . . . the performance had due vigour and vividness. For this much of the credit belongs with ANN HOWARD's Carmen, whose sexiness resides as much in the colour of her voice as in the swirl of her skirt. And it is not easy to think of any other Carmen who looks the part so fully.

Stanley Sadie—THE TIMES March 13 1974

Carmen must be a sex symbol. The whole opera, after all, is littered with those blighted Spaniards who have succumbed to her charms at the mere flick of a coolly-dropped flower. ANN HOWARD's earthy temptress is a very sexy lady indeed. If Carmen was the original dropout then the liberal cut of Miss Howard's dresses suggest she is taking the description literally. Her performance, however, is rather subtler than the dresses, hinting at a somewhat sullied purity behind the flippant and passionate facade. In strong vocal form, too, ...

David Gillard—DAILY MAIL March 16 1974

Changes of cast during the current revival brought back to this stage (The London Coliseum) . . . ANN HOWARD's Carmen – still the most striking performance of the role by a British mezzo in many years, the only one to capture in any degree both the toughness and the sensuality by means convincingly physical as well as vocal . . .

Max Loppert—THE FINANCIAL TIMES March 14 1974

ANN HOWARD is really splendid in the tomboy or Olga Nethersole tradition and very natural seeming, full of life, and full in voice, at times really impressive in the sense of a good reserve. As English Carmens rate she has no difficulty in making the language sound easy and clear. One did not all the time miss the cut of the French.

Philip Hope-Wallace—THE GUARDIAN March 13 1974

In tall, lissom, hip-swaying ANN HOWARD there is the supreme amalgam of operatic fulfilment – a Carmen who seduces the senses in every respect. And behind the exotic, exulting bravura of this extrovert character she manages to capture sympathy in the sad inevitability of her doom.

Ronald Wilkinson—reviewing THE LEEDS GRAND THEATRE

<u>Revival at the London Coliseum 1978</u>

Entitled 'Vibrant 'Carmen' is sharply observed'

Among several mid-run cast changes in 'Carmen' at the Coliseum is the return of ANN HOWARD to the title role in which she made so memorable an impression when John Copley's still fresh, still enormously striking production was first staged eight years ago. A major strength of her performance is that it seems to grow naturally out of, and is throughout consistently related to, Carmen's frequently stated need to feel absolutely free of restraint, even in love. With the core of her personality so decisively established, the gradual emergence of the almost wilfully fatalistic side of her nature has both a plausible and almost desperate inevitability. This emergence of her darker side from the teasing lightness and vivacity of the opening scenes comes when her freedom is threatened.

And, in splendid rich and vibrant voice, MISS HOWARD matched sharp observation of character with singing on Wednesday (April 12 1978) that moved effortlessly from carefree allure and sensuality to fervently expressed passion.

Robert Henderson—THE DAILY TELEGRAPH—April 14th 1978

Also of the 1978 revival:

ANN HOWARD makes a handsome, full-voiced and vigorous heroine, especially good at carrying along the taxing second act. MISS HOWARD in particular earns some sort of recognition as an English Carmen making the point for new visitors to such a world. Many school children and foreign visitors were getting the message with obvious enjoyment.

Phiip Hope-Wallace—THE GUARDIAN April 14 1978

Also of the 1978 revival

Entitled 'A dominating heroine'

. . . this revival boasts a central performance by ANN HOWARD which puts most of her colleagues to shame. Physically she dominates the stage, and not only by reason of her imposing height; from her first entrance she is, indisputably, the leader of the pack, the bodily focus for this drama of sex and death. Her vocal contribution is no less impressive. Not so husky as she has been sometimes in the past, she commands a range of tone that extends from the rich and creamy to an enticing smokiness and then to a mocking snarl that would be enough to emasculate the bravest suitor.

Paul Griffiths—THE TIMES April 13 1978

Press reviews from Carmen performances in other countries.

Municipal Auditorium, New Orleans 197

The New Orleans Opera House Association was the sponsoring agent for the American debut of the leading lady, Ann Howard, a British mezzo-soprano who has had success with the title role at the Sadler's Wells Opera. She was an emphatic hit here too, performing with appealing verve in the framework of guest stage direction by Bliss Hebert. Friday's audience saluted the first New Orleans performance of Don Jose by Placido Domingo . . . .

The Fort Worth Star-Telegram, Dallas, reported on an interview with Ann about her interpretation of the role of Carmen.

The British singer spoke about her impressions of the role. "I think she is obviously a sex symbol, but not in a negative way. I find her enormously natural, instinctive, high-spirited and I like to play the role with a sense of humor, very quick, spontaneously. I don't think you should have a bad feeling about her at the end. After all, she did warn Don Jose that he shouldn't get too interested. She doesn't lead him on or purposely try to hurt him. He just gets too possessive and she rebels. She feels trapped, and I believe she really loves him in her own way. If he would just leave well enough alone I think he would have her much longer. But he can't, and she has to move on. Escamillo (the bull fighter) is the way out. I don't think it ever enters her head, despite the fortune telling, that don Jose might harm her. Even at the end I think she thinks he's bluffing, that he won't go through with it. And that is her downfall.

Leonard Eureka FORT WORTH STAR-TELEGRAM December 3 1976

(See below the review written the next day written by Leonard Eureka)

'Carmen' can't work without a believable title character. English mezzo-soprano ANN HOWARD was more than believable, she was a revelation. A tall, striking, buxom woman, Miss Howard was one of the rare Carmens to have the physical allure and sensuality the character calls for. She also possesses a big, multi-colored voice that she uses with intelligence. It may not be the most beautiful voice ever heard in the part, but it was consistently interesting and under superb control.

What made Miss Howard's Carmen so vital was her mastery of the little things – the winks, the gestures, the brassy walk – that delineate the character. I don't know what else she can sing, but if she does it all this well she ought to have a sensational career.

Mark Melson—THE SHREVEPORT TIMES December 10 1976

Review of the Fort Worth (Dallas) performance Tarrant County Convention Centre Theatre 1976

ANN HOWARD is a deathless Carmen, Bizet's bad girl of grand opera. Some Carmen portrayers make you wonder what the fuss is all about. Ms. Howard almost pulls you onto the stage into the action.

Vocally, she is completely acceptable. There are no induced growls in the low regions, the voice lies very naturally in the role. The edge of the voice is not normally heard in the role, but this is by no means a vocal fault. Consequently, Carmen's highlight is not a caressing Habanera nor a brooding Card Song, but a challenging and flip Seguidilla.

Entitled 'Carmen. Heroine radiant in opener'

A full house greeted the Fort Worth Opera's opening production of 'Carmen' (on) Friday at (the) Tarrant County Convention Centre Theatre. And little wonder. With a Carmen like this (ANN HOWARD) and a production as attractive as this, who wouldn't want to be there?

Ms. Howard looks and sounds like a million dollars, and her sympathy for the role seems total. Hers is not a cardboard, paste-up version of the Bizet heroine, but a blood-and-thunder human being who lives life to the full and doesn't quite understand people who don't.

Leonard Eureka—STAR-TELEGRAM Fort Worth December 4 1976

Re: the Carmen production in Guadalajara, Mexico 1978

Entitled 'Stop the Opera and on with the Bullfight' A Unique Last Act!

British opera star ANN HOWARD was flattered when a Mexican producer invited her to sing Bizet's Carmen in far-off Guadalajara. She was in New York singing Carmen last month when the Mexican – a singer called Franco Inglesias – offered her the star part in his new production.

She accepted, but nearly choked over her celebratory glass of tequila when Senor Iglesias revealed that his Carmen is to be staged in a 6,000-seater bull ring – with a real, full-scale bull-fight in the last act. But he explained that the stage would be built at the side of the bullring and the opera would be stopped so that the bull fight could take place.

When the toreador Escamillo leaves Carmen to go to the bull fight the opera will temporarily come to a halt, and a real fight will be staged in the ring . . . . says Miss Howard: I understand it will be a very glamorous and spectacular affair with a full procession, a band and professional matadors and picadors. (Read Ann's tale of the performance in the 'Wall of Death' chapter.)

New York City Opera production November 1972

Miss Howard, who made her City Opera debut as Carmen two weeks ago, began well simply by looking so gorgeous. She brought a deliciously off-hand je m'en fiche attitude to the character – a high-spirited girl living to the hilt until Jose becomes uncooperative and spoils it all. Miss Howard carried this approach off with real flair and her scenes with Jose (Harry Theyard) crackled with give-and-take electricity.

Peter G. Davis—THE NEW YORK TIMES November 13 1972

Monday's colourful production of Carmen was sparked by the admirable voice of Placido Domingo as Don Jose and the brilliant acting and singing of contralto ANN HOWARD in the title role.

R.W.Stiles—PASADENA STAR-NEWS November 26 1972

ANN HOWARD' the New York City Opera guest Carmen, is pretty and playful. She does the first two acts barefoot, teases anyone in sight, and capitalizes on incidental dramatic subtleties. She asks, rather politely, that an audience pay attention to her; the rewards are many, but easily missed – at least in 'Carmen'

There are a lot of things that this fall British mezzo doesn't do – fortunately. She doesn't try for more hip-waving sultriness than she can reasonably carry off. She doesn't panic. Hers is a human Carmen, life-sized, spunky and vulnerable.

Miss Howard is singing three Carmens this season with three different Don Joses. Her first was none less than Placido Domingo who flew down from San Francisco for one performance . . .

Karen Monson—LOS ANGELES HERALD-EXAMINER November 22 1972

America Calling

Ann was, at this time, a member of the ENO company. She worked for other organisations, but her first call would always have to be for them. Marguerita Stafford, an agent in England who had colleagues in America and Europe, had been taking an interest in Ann's growing career. She acted for Plácido Domingo who was singing roles in the United States. Domingo saw Ann's performance and immediately recommended her for work in the USA. Within quite a short while, Ann found herself invited to sing Carmen for the New company. She worked for other organizations, but her first call would always have to be for them. Marguerita Stafford, an agent in England who had colleagues in America and Europe, had been taking an interest in Ann's growing career. She acted for Plácido Domingo who was singing roles in the United States. Domingo saw Ann's performance and immediately recommended her for work in the USA. Within quite a short while, Ann found herself invited to sing Carmen for the New York City Opera and also for the New Orleans Opera. She was to sing the role with Domingo as Don José on a number of occasions.

Until I jogged her memory, Ann did not speak of the fact that she sang Carmen in English, and that these new dates would often require her to sing it in the original French. It is no small undertaking to re-learn a role in another language. Few people realise how extremely hard an opera singer has to work. There were times when both English and French productions were being performed close together, requiring a feat of memory. Ann readily admits that she worked hard, but always with the caveat that she enjoyed it all. 'I always take my scores to bed with me.' She confided. 'It's there in your head all night'.

So, an international career now beckoned, but her engagements in Britain still came thick and fast. In June she was in Bath with the BBC rehearsing, and eventually performing, Beethoven's Ninth Symphony. Even while *Carmen* was still in rehearsal, on March 1st she took part in Weber's *Oberon* at a BBC broadcast performance in the Royal Festival Hall with Alberto Remedios and Joan Carlyle. In October of this year she particularly remembers that she started singing in concerts with Arthur Blake ('a lovely man'). She was to continue doing so for many years. Blake was the head of music for Scottish Television and he conducted regular studio performances with a small invited audience. Ann could sing the songs from operetta and shows that she loved – even certain 'pop' songs – and she greatly enjoyed herself.

ENO then embarked on a new venture: to mount the musical *Kiss Me Kate*. For Ann this was great news as her first love had always been for musicals. She remembers it with great affection. She played the principal female role of Lilly Vanessi. This was sheer theatrical glamour which included having a full-sized portrait of her displayed outside the Coliseum. It opened on December 24th 1970.

Top Left: 'Kiss Me Kate': Ann as Lilly Vanessi with Emile Belcourt 1969 Photo: Donald Southern

Bottom Left: 'Kiss Me Kate' Ann sings 'So In Love'

Below: 'Kiss Me Kate': Ann with Emile Belcourt singing 'Wunderbar' Photo: Donald Southern

PRESS

Kiss me Kate by Cole Porter

Entitled: 'Poor old Kate should have been left at home . . .

Adapting this once-Famous American musical to the resources of a major opera company is like putting a quart into a pint pot . . . . . Not new enough to repeat its first impact (1951, 20 years ago); not old enough to acquire a patina of period charm, the show is less for the young at heart than the middle-aged in spirit.

ANN HOWARD, more familiar as an excellent Carmen, makes much of the Lilli Vanessi role by rich-voiced singing and her own brand of bold enthusiasm.

Noel Goodwin—DAILY EXPRESS December 28 1970

Whether or not Sadler's Wells was wise in its choice of Cole Porter's 'Kiss Me Kate' for its Christmas production must . . . . be merely of academic interest. For there the show is, and it offers many incidental pleasures . . . . And it appeals to one's natural sense of symmetry that 'Kiss Me Kate', whose first London performance was at the Coliseum, should be back in the same theatre almost exactly 20 years later. Except on a few occasions, however, it never quite manages to catch the very distinctive accent of the American musical at itw most vivacious and ebullient.

And yet I still think the choice was a wise one even if the experiment hasn't quite succeeded. The musical in its brilliant upsurge of creative activity in the late forties is as much an authentic expression of the American spirit at its best and at its most characteristic as 'The Merry Widow' of the Vienna of Franz Joseph or Offenbach of 'Las Belle Epoque'. And among musicals 'Kiss Me Kate' occupies a very special place, both for its witty, toughly-written book and its astonishing succession of memorable songs, almost every one of which has long since become a Denmark Street 'standard'.

The performance has all the necessary zest and exhilaration, but presented with an essentially English, and in the context totally unidiomatic reserve, lacking that kind of irrepressible optimism and self-generating spontaneity which, as so many American companies have already shown us, are not incompatible with immaculate polish and a faultless precision down to the tiniest detail.

Robert Henderson—THE SUNDAY TELEGRAPH January 3 1971

ANN HOWARD makes a strong-voiced shrew any red-blooded man would love to tame.

Eric Mason—DAILY MAIL December 28 1970

The transmogrification of this classic musical into something very near a light opera need disturb the partisans of neither school. Cole Porter's melodies sound all the better for the disciplined singing of the Sadler's Wells principals, and Emile Belcourt and ANN HOWARD as Petruchio and Katherine and their 20th-century analogues act with more subtlety than one habitually expects from operatic (or even musical comedy) companies.

B.A. Young—THE FINANCIAL TIMES December 28 1970

ANN HOWARD, last season's Carmen, has a physical resemblance to Elizabeth Taylor and her shrew scenes reminds one of that lady in the film The Taming Of The Shrew. She sings strongly and the whole performance is full of spirit.

Sydney Edwards—December 28 1970

ANN HOWARD is excellent as Lilli Vanessi, a shrew in real life as well as on stage. She sings charmingly, she creates a strong character, she fascinates with her 'temperaments'.

THE STAGE December 31 1970

. . . I am less concerned with whether or not our second opera house should have any truck with Cole Porter and musical comedy and more with registering profound admiration at its versatility . . . . ANN HOWARD as Lilli Vanessi and Emile Belcourt as her ex-husband project their love-hate relationship very engagingly.

Unaccustomed as I am to electronic amplification of a perfectly adequate natural level of vocal and instrumental performance, I found the first night decibals deafening. And I will never reconcile myself to seeing a singer on one side of the stage and hearing her voice through a loud-speaker on the other side . . . . a colleague, more at home in cabaret than opera house found the show lacking in zing and zest I experienced. This, I think, is largely a matter of those decibels.

Felix Aprahamian—THE TIMES January 3 1971

From Wagner to The Good Old days

1971

Ann's schedule began January 3rd with *Sunday Night at The Coliseum* for the BBC. Work with the BBC threaded itself through Ann's career. At that time the BBC had several staff orchestras which specialised in Light Music. Programmes of this popular genre were broadcast every day, often as live performances. *Grand Hotel* and *Friday Night Is Music Night* were regulars and these always required singers. If the BBC needed a mezzo soprano, Ann was invited.

The BBC also promoted performances of opera for radio and must take credit for giving performances of many neglected works. At the end of January Ann played a part in *La Fille de Madame Argot* by Lecocq and later in the year Janáček's *Osud*. It is interesting to note that in the short time since she returned from studying in Paris, as well as these two operas she had taken part in *The Arcadians, Cendrillon, The Mock doctor, Mavra, Ulysses* and *The Kiss.* In early 1972 she sang a role in *The Nose* by Shostakovitch. A number of these productions were broadcast from Manchester under the direction of Edward Downes. Television performances were far rarer, though she played Orlovsky in *Die Fledermaus* in a lovely production which the BBC filmed later in the year.

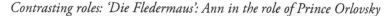

Contrasting roles: 'Die Fledermaus': Ann in the role of Prince Orlovsky

Ann as Ortrud in 'Lohengrin' by Wagner

Ann as Prince Orlovsky singing the famous aria 'Chacun a son Goût'
in the televised production of 'Die Fledermaus' by Johann Strauss
Photos: BBC copyright

A holiday was needed, but work soon recommenced with rehearsals for a second run of *Kiss Me Kate* which opened on July 17th. Another Wagner opera was also in the making: *Lohengrin* – Ann to sing the role of Ortrud ('That was a hard part.') This opened on August 12th and was followed by a further seven performances until the end of October. *Carmen* returned. In one week Ann sang *Lohengrin* on Thursday and in *Carmen* on Saturday – two completely different roles in close proximity. A further change of style came as *Iolanthe* was revived in late October. *Aïda*, in which Ann was to sing the role of Amneris began. This schedule was extremely challenging both vocally and physically.

1972

Now an exceptionally busy singer in Britain, Ann's career in America started to take off. Her earlier performances in New Orleans and New York had introduced her to several other opera houses. In late August of this year she flew to Toronto to begin rehearsals of Verdi's *Aïda*, to sing the role of Amneris. Performances there commenced on September 19th and continued into mid-October. She then flew to New York to sing *Carmen* and soon afterwards to Los Angeles with the New York City Opera

A new run of both *Carmen* and *The Valkyrie* began in February and March, involving fresh rehearsals. These operas demanded a quite separate style which required a measure of versatility.

On April 11th she flew to New Orleans. After only two rehearsals gave two performances of *Carmen*. It was her USA debut. She returned home to continue with *The Valkyrie* in London and begin a tour with *Carmen* which took her to Manchester, Leeds and Newcastle. 'The tour went on forever,' she commented.

Also during this year her home life saw an important development. With daughter Katherine now four years old, Keith and Ann purchased a bigger house. They had lived in Surbiton since their marriage and now they moved only a few yards away into the handsome house which has remained Ann's home until the present day. Here there was accommodation for a nanny for Katherine, and a comfortable home to return to after singing in London or abroad.

Left: Ann at home: (No 56) 'Prima Donna Domestica' – Ann loves cooking
Above: (No 57) Ann with daughter Katherine   Photos: United Press International

1973

Samson and Dalila returned for Ann, this time performances in the original French in Nancy, France, which began in late January. She returned home to start to learn and rehearsal the role of Brangäne in Wagner's *Tristan and Isolde* for Scottish Opera. Ann described this as a most difficult and nerve-wracking role. The tessitura is high for a mezzo soprano and has to be sung very often off-stage. It is also a most heart-rending love story which often reduced Ann to tears on stage; indeed this was the only opera that caused her to weep in this way. The first night was in Glasgow on May 5th followed by a tour to Edinburgh and Aberdeen.

Scottish Opera's 'Tristan and Isolde' by Wagner. Ann in the role of Brangäne

At the same time she was in the ENO production of *The Rheingold* which was being performed in Liverpool. The 'English Ring' was now in full performance during the summer months. Ann sang in *The Rhinegold* and *The Valkyrie*, and she was occasionally required (by conductor Reginald Goodall) to sing the part of a Norn in *Twilight of the Gods*.

This diet of tragic, grand opera was offset for Ann by performing in the televised *The Good Old Days* in which she sang 'Just a song at twilight'. This was a very popular show in which the audience dressed in Edwardian costume to give it a true Music Hall ambiance. It was filmed in the City Varieties Theatre in Leeds. (Leeds had four theaties in those days.) She also sang in the BBC broadcast of *Music for Pleasure* and for STV with Arthur Blake, a televised programme of light music called *The Melody Lingers On*. Frequently these different engagements occurred on consecutive days, sometimes necessitating a journey to Scotland and back.

In September English National Opera North's production of Richard Rodney Bennett's *The Mines Of Sulphur* went into rehearsal to be conducted by David Lloyd Jones. Ann revived the role that she had sung in 1966 in London. Rehearsals also started on Janáček's *Katya Kabanova* and (for BBC TV) Verdi's *La traviata*.

Throughout the rest of her career Ann was to sing Carmen in many different opera houses throughout Europe and America. These performances were always in French; only with ENO did she sing it in English. In October of this year she was in San Diego and Phoenix. ('That was really hot'). As she had successfully sung with New York City Opera she was now in demand in many other cities.

She returned to continue rehearsals for the BBC's televised *La Traviata*. Ann had a small role but the main roles were taken by the principal singers of ENO: John Brecknock, Elizabeth Harwood and Norman Bailey. Alan Opie and Philip Langridge had smaller roles with Ann playing Flora ('the usual tarty friend). She remembers it as a 'beautiful production' The year ended with a BBC *Music For Your Pleasure* with Barrie Knight.

1974

'The Offenbachs were very, very good for me. They were always much more fun than anything. I just loved doing them – loved doing them'. Ann was truly happy to be working on an Offenbach opera at this time: *Bluebear*d with rehearsals commencing in January. Her role – that of Boulotte, the leading female character – was charming and comic; she also has happy memories of working with John Brecknock, the tenor, who was

enjoying his first big success. She was later to sing in other Offenbach operas: *La Belle Helene, The Grand Duchess of Gerolstein* and *Orpheus in the Underworld*. All of these had a leading role for Ann. Offenbach had always composed his operas with a particular singer in mind. In this case it was Hortense Schneider whose voice-type must have been exactly like Ann's.

Cartoon: Jonathan Miller by 'High'

Later in the same month she met two people who were to lay a big part in her future career: Mary Nash, the repetiteur and Jonathan Miller. The meeting was in Mary's house where an introductory rehearsal for a contemporary opera by Alexander Goehr, *Arden Must*

Die, was taking place. Jonathan Miller was to produce this opera with his usual panache for The New Opera Company. Mary Nash became Ann's chief repetiteur. This professional relationship with Mary turned into a close personal friendship, and continues to this day

Leaving all this in England Ann went to Calgary, Canada, to sing *Carmen*. She stayed for two weeks, returning to do *Invitation To Music* for the BBC at the Golders Green Hippodrome and to commence rehearsals on Prokofiev's *War and Peace*. In March rehearsals began in earnest for *Arden Must Die* – Ann playing the part of Mrs Arden.

PRESS

Press reviews of ARDEN MUST DIE by Alexander Goehr. NEW OPERA COMPANY production at Sadler's Wells theatre, April 1974

There I discovered much to intrigue and delight the ear and mind . . . . within the limitations of their resources the New Opera Company's performance was distinctly creditable, with notable contributions from ANN HOWARD (Alice – Mrs Arden), John Cameron (Arden) and Nigel Rogers (Mosbie). Jonathan Miller's Maria Marten-style of production neatly emphasised the work's grotesque flavour . . .

Peter Heyworth—THE OBSERVER April 21 1974

Headed 'Must Opera Die?'

For those who relish such things, there was a certain gruesome chill about the messy details of the murder. There were also good performances from ANN HOWARD as the Lady Macbeth of the Kentish Weald . . . .

Desmond Shawe-Taylor—THE SUNDAY TIMES April 21 1974

The large and excellent cast was led by ANN HOWARD and Nigel Rogers as the wicked pair.

Peter Stadlen—THE DAILY TELEGRAPH April 18 1974

Santa Fe 'like nothing else'

The Santa Fe Opera of Offenbach's opera 'The Grand Duchess of Gerolstein' ann in the title role

The last three months of this opera season were extremely busy. The BBC were preparing to perform *Armide* by Gluck in which Ann had a role and work on *Arden Must Die* continued. A further performance of The English Ring took place. Then, just a month before Ann's 40th birthday she flew to America to perform in the Santa Fe Opera.

Many people have a glamorous idea of opera: the wonderful music – the exotic costumes – the famous people in the audience and the charmed life of the opera stars. Little of this is true for most of the time; behind each performance is hours of work and long rehearsals. But in Santa Fe perhaps the dream is almost true. Ann described it as 'like nothing else – a marvellous experience.' It was the brain-child of millionaire John Crosby who adored opera and conducted some of the performances. Perhaps it could be compared with Glyndebourne as it attracted a large and wealthy audience and was therefore financially as well as artistically successful. It continues until the present day.

Santa Fe is situated in a dramatic desert setting with a backdrop of mountains. Ann described how breathtakingly beautiful the mountains become at night when the setting sun turns them a terracotta colour against a deep blue sky. The operas take full advantage of this in their productions as the opera stage has no back wall.

The principal singers were given lovely houses to live in and Ann was able to be joined by Keith and Katherine. The opera grounds contained a swimming pool and an excellent restaurant, all truly luxurious and a far cry from touring in the north of England and Scotland. (Well, there was one drawback: one had to beware of the rattle snakes.)

Santa Fe Opera: 'The Grand Duchess of Gerolstein' Photo: Robert C. Ragsdale

The Offenbach was to be the opening performance of the festival, and was to enjoy a brilliant production. Ann told me that the chorus was particularly impressive. It was made up of about 50 young singers drawn from all over America. They had been auditioned throughout the previous year and they were able to both sing and dance brilliantly or take minor roles. It was part of Crosby's policy to give young singers a good professional experience to boost their careers.

Ann went to Santa Fe five times in all and has the happiest memories of it. She is quick to say that it was not a holiday as a great deal of work went into the preparation and performances of the operas, but there was a marvellously happy atmosphere among the participants. The parties were truly memorable as they had various original and comic themes. For some, the guests had to turn up wearing the clothes that they had on when they received the invitation – which might be night attire or just a bath towel. Another was the 'No Taste' party which produced some quite unmentionable costumes.

She arrived there on June 27th to commence a month of rehearsal. This comparatively long period meant that there was no undue pressure and life could include nightly parties and socialising. There were three stages and the rehearsals took place on the stage of the eventual performance: a great advantage. Each principal singer had a main role and a smaller role in another opera. Ann was to sing the title role in *La Grande Duchesse* (Offenbach) and a part in *L'Egisto* by Cavalli.

Santa Fe Opera: Ann as the Grand Duchess of Gerolstein

She returned from Santa Fe on August 25th to take up her work with Mary Nash on *Arden Must Die* and the role of Amneris in *Aïda*. A few weeks later she was in Milwaukee to sing the latter part. The remaining months of the year found her travelling to and from foreign parts: Edmonton, Canada to sing *Carmen* and Rouen in France to sing Delilah – now, for the first time – in French.

Pic. No 66

1975

Pic. No. 112

It is no small labour to re-learn a role in another language. In the early part of this year Ann was working with the conductor Anthony Hose on an English version of *The Grand Duchess* which Ann had sung in French at Santa Fe. This was for performances with the Welsh National Opera with a completely new production by Malcolm Frazer. Rehearsals took place in Cardiff and the opera opened in Fishguard on March 4th. A tour followed, visiting Aberystwyth, Leicester, Cardiff, Swansea, Brighton (Theatre Royal) and Wolverhampton.

Pic. No. 67

An extraordinary few days occurred commencing with the performance of *The Grand Duchess* in Wolverhampton on May 20th. She then flew to Rouen in France to sing Delilah on May 21st, with a further performance of *Samson and Delilah* in Caen on May 23rd, returning to Wolverhampton to sing *The Grand Duchess* on May 24th. Unlike other 'close encounters' like this she was singing principal roles in both of these operas and both were entirely different in style and content.

Ann's career was now firmly established in Britain, America and France. The roles of Carmen, Delilah, Fricka, The Grand Duchess and the Witch in *Hansel and Gretel* were set to be performed for various opera companies over the ensuing years, interlaced with engagements with the BBC.

A publicity stunt in Cardiff to promote Welsh National Opera's production of 'The Grand Duchess of Gerolstein'. Yes – he was a real policeman.

1976

At this point in the appointments diary some entries stating 'coat' had to be explained. They were for fittings for a fabulous mink coat which was being made for her by a firm in Bond Street: a gift from Ann's proud father.

In May ,while rehearsing Belle Helene in Sunderland, Ann attended a performance with Ann Hood in the leading role. Ms. Hood became ill after the first act and Ann sang her role from the wings. In the following weeks Ann followed the ENO tour around, rehearsing the roles she was to do in London: Carmen and Belle Hélène. She found herself in Liverpool ,Wolverhampton and Cardiff.

In July she was in a BBC production of *Hansel and Gretel*. Her outstanding memory of this was of being on a 'Chopper' bike (a Modernist idea of a broomstick) during a rehearsal . She was suspended a few feet in the air awaiting an entry from the wings. A young man greeted her from below, and she said 'Oh, I am just hanging about' Later she realised that this young man was HRH Prince Andrew.

By May Ann was having regular rehearsals with Mary Nash for the starring role in *The Italian Girl in Algiers* by Rossini. This was a new adventure for Ann, being very florid with much coloratura to learn. She remembers that it was a comic role, very hard, but she loved it. She was to go to Baltimore later to perform it.

'The Italian girl in Algiers' by Rossini

1977

During leisure moments in Bordeaux Ann met two Italian singers who taught her a wonderful card game with two pack and four Jokers. She still plays it to this day quite regularly with Mary Nash and other friends. Ann has a life-long love of card games.

1978

We commenced this part of Ann's history with a discussion on being a mezzo soprano in opera. She agreed that the public's conception of an opera diva was almost invariably a soprano, not a mezzo. She rather ruefully commented that the mezzo role in an opera is often more difficult than the soprano role, but less celebrated. All the heroines of Verdi and Puccini are sopranos playing the parts of lovers to the principal male role – (usually a tenor). Of course there are exceptions, and Ann played all the principal mezzo roles in the course of her career – notably Carmen and Delilah and the Offenbach roles. These roles are often rich in dramatic possibilities – comic, or tragic, or wonderfully wicked (those 'witches and bitches' again) and many are mature or older women's roles which can be convincingly performed by a singer in the latter part of her career.

April 29th: BBC concert in the Royal Festival Hall

Ann recalls that she met two interesting and famous people from the world of stage musicals at this BBC concert: Sally Ann Howes and Evelyn Laye. She greatly enjoyed talking to both of them. Did she still harbour a wish to go on to the West End stage in a musical? In the course of our conversations this topic often crops up. She had had a near miss with *My Fair Lady* when she got the cover part for Eliza Doolittle back in the days before opera filled her life. The nearest she gets to that world now is in concerts and broadcasts for the BBC where show songs are performed.

May 25th. Interview at the Holborn Library for the Opera Club. Ann spoke about her career to Tom Higgins who then accompanied her to sing 'Love Went a Riding' by Frank Bridge. This was the very same song that she had sung to Jack Waller in 1956 which had led to the beginning of her professional career on the stage. Ann was beginning to be well known in the opera world. This interview was the second within a month.

Pic. No. 113

For a few weeks Ann's diary is not full of performances. One might hope that she was relaxing, meeting up with friends and enjoying her domestic life in Surbiton; but, as she often pointed out to me, these 'bare patches' were often times for learning roles and working with Mary Nash. However, in May she was in Mexico singing *Carmen* and in July in Vichy, France, also for *Carmen*. On returning to London she started rehearsals for the role of Preziosilla in Verdi's opera *The Force of Destiny*.

Many rehearsals ensued for *The Force of Destiny* and further performances of *Carmen* were planned. However a dispute between the management of ENO and the chorus led to a total change of plan. The dispute led to a strike which meant that the *Carmen* performances had to be cancelled and *The Force of Destiny* put on hold. The decision was taken to perform Menotti's masterpiece *The Consul* as this has no chorus. All of the people who were to sing *Carmen* got roles for *The Consul*; Ann had the role of The Secretary. ('A lovely part, that was'). *The Consul* took over all the cancelled *Carmen* performances.

The first night of *The Consul was on August 12*[th]. Ann's diary is illustrated with a skull and crossbones and two exclamation marks on this date. Could this be because the rehearsal time had been remarkably short?

Ann in the role of The Secretary (right) in Menotti's opera 'The Consul' with Shelagh Squires as Magda
Photo: Mike Humphrey

In September and October Ann was learning and rehearsing the pivotal role of Eboli in Verdi's *Don Carlos* for a performance in Baltimore, USA. This long rehearsal period was welcomed by Ann as this was a new opera for her and a new part to sing. She described it as wonderful with a beautiful aria near the beginning, but very difficult with a high tessitura. ('A killer'). Indeed, when she was offered the role she initially refused it, but the company insisted that they really wanted her. Ann negotiated that Eboli's main aria 'O don fatale' which is written in the high soprano range, be transposed down a semitone.

1979

In the last few sessions our conversations have been based on Ann's appointment diaries for these busy years in the 1970s. What can one glean about a life from such information? Certainly one reads here about an exceptionally full schedule of work: learning sessions with a repetiteur, (mostly with Mary Nash), rehearsals, performances, travel. There are references to social occasions too, especially in Santa Fe where a circle of friends was building up and from home there is news of the young Katherine's activities. The diary never tells how Ann is feeling.

As we speak she fills in the gaps, often remembering an amusing incident or recalling a long-lost friend or fellow singer. Almost without exception these memories are of happy times and of her enjoyment of each new challenge. She is often amazed at the sheer volume of work and wonders how she managed it all, stating that she always felt well – and only had to cancel three or four performances in her whole career.

*This page and the next page: English National Opera North's production o
'Hansel and Gretel' by Humpeerdinck – Ann as the Witch*

CHAPTER 8

'I Don't Know How I Did It'

1979

The schedule in January entailed popping up and down from London to Leeds on an almost daily basis.

Ann was to sing in several different productions of *Hansel and Gretel* during her career – playing the part of the Witch. The first time was for Sadler's Wells at the age of 26 ('A nasty old witch with a false nose'). With ENON she was a very glamorous Witch with a beautiful ball gown (though a closer inspection would reveal that it was decorated with frogs and spiders and other unpleasant artefacts), and later there was the 'Chopper' bicycle experience for television. Speaking of the role, Ann said that it was Wagnerian in character and had a very wide range – cackling on a top B one minute and plunging down the next. Ann relished these 'wicked' parts.

In January she travelled to Toledo, Ohio to rehearse *Carmen* for a performance at the end of the month. Ann's dresser in Toledo was a German lady who became a lifelong friend. She came from Munich and later, when Ann performed there, she sent her beautiful flowers from America. She had a young son who was put on stage in the performances of *Samson and Delilah* to show Samson to the pillars in the last act. This little boy grew up to become the Administrator of the Chicago Lyric Opera Company.

A further run of *Carmen* with ENO at the London Coliseum had its first night on February 1st, though the night before Ann had been in Hull for a performance of Hansel and Gretel with ENON. Then, with the ENON tour continuing through February, new rehearsals for Wagner's *Ring* commenced with a couple of *Carmen*s thrown in for good measure In the middle of March she travelled to Naples for *The Rhinegold*: an astonishing period of work.

Keith and Katherine had joined Ann in Naples. However, as they went on to Rome for a holiday, Ann received a surprise telephone call from her agent telling her to go to Montreal at once to sing *Carmen*. So she travelled back to London on her own, picked up her wigs and make up and left at once for Canada.

The performances were on April 20 and 21 and Ann's abiding memory is that she hated the costume. She returned to a busy Spring in London then set off for Santa Fe on June 13 to rehearse and perform another run of *The Grand Duchess of Geroldstein.*

English National Opera glitterati. From left: Lord Harewood, Ann Howard, Dennis Dowling, Ava June, Geoffrey Chard, Alberto Remedios, Harold Rosenthal, Mark Elder,an unknown person, Lord Goodman and Harry Blackburn

1980

From the very beginning of this year Ann was performing in a number of operas both in Britain and France: *Die Fledermaus, Hansel and Gretel, Carmen* and *The Mines of Sulphur*. By early Spring she was involved with both *The Mines of Sulphur* for ENON in Leeds and performances of *The Ring* in Bristol for ENO, sometimes on consecutive days. The remembrance of this hectic period made her exclaim, 'I don't know how I did it'. In May and June she was in Ghent with *Samson and Delilah*, and then, in July, she travelled to Pretoria, South Africa.

Ann remembers that she stayed in a hotel right on the beach near Pretoria. Keith and Katherine joined her there. One evening, she and a friend had an enjoyable swim in the sea. When she mentioned this to the hotel staff they informed her that these waters were infested with sharks. In August, Ann was in Johannesburg for further performances of *Carmen*.

Ann, with conductor David de Villiers, were awarded the honour of being the 33rd and 34th 'arts' people to imprint their hands and signatures on cement tiles at the Johannesburg Civic Theatre

At this point we spoke about the business side of being an international opera singer. I enquired about the costs of going to a foreign country, sometimes for only one performance. A singer would be paid for a performance, but out of this fee would have to come the expenses of travel, fees to the agent and to repetiteurs and hotel and living expenses. The fee might be a considerable sum, certainly over a thousand pounds, but much of this would have to be spent on expenses. Happily for Ann, all of this was organised by her agent. Husband Keith was also there to help manage her career, not least of all to meet her at various airports and railway stations.

PRESS

Carmen in South Africa/Canada/Scotland

<u>Performance in the Civic Theatre, Johannesburg;</u>

Ann Howard, a mezzo soprano, has a rich voice and personality. She did not make the mistake of turning Carmen into a totally disreputable person, but through her acting captured the voluptuousness of the character.

Michael Traub—THE CITIZEN September 1 1980

Traub also commented that the Don Jose (Franco Bonanome) was a substitute, called in as Richard Kness was indisposed. He could only sing the role in French though the company was singing in an English translation. He wrote: The Carmen, English star Ann Howard, wisely switched to French in all her confrontations with Don Jose and retained English vis-a-vis the general cast.

<u>Of the same production</u>

In the title role is English mezzo-soprano Ann Howard – sultry, seductive and vicious.'

Michael Calenborne—PRETORIA NEWS August 13 1980

Her (Ann Howard's) voice is strong and full, more of a contralto than a true mezzo, and her words were always carried across on her tones. Intelligent acting was always present and she knew how to use her very attractive features and certainly made the most use of her eyes. She portrayed the quick-tempered and temperamental gypsy with great verve and in her scene in the tavern with don Jose she ran the gamut of emotion..

Harol Steafel—RAND DAILY MAIL August 30 1980

If you can imagine Racquel Welch with a voice, which I am sure you can, then you have a close approximation to Ann Howard. She was the most magnificent, voluptuous Carmen seen here in years. A splendid, warm, earthy voice, a fine stage presence and considerable acting ability and with a figure to match, Ann Howard had all the attributes to make this role a memorable one.

John Davies—THE STAR September 2 1980

Press review of ENON performance in Glasgow, April 1980.

Much of the opera's impact is due to the singing and acting ability of Ann Howard in the title role. She presents Carmen as a smouldering tigress both in her vocal power and in the earthiness of her acting. It is a memorable and strong performance which makes the whole opera credible. For one can understand the sheer animal vitality which makes men Carmen's willing victims.

Janet Beat—THE SCOTSMAN April 16 1980

Alberta Opera production in Calgary. February 1974

Londoner Ann Howard has all the attributes to be remembered as one of the great Carmens of our time. As ravishing visually as she was vocally, she dominated the stage from her initial entrance. She possesses a rich and resourceful mezzo voice, but add to this a stunning stage presence, unmistakable acting gifts, and a shrewd understanding of her character's nature,and you have something very special.

Jamie Portman February 1974

<u>Southern Alberta Opera Association production .Calgary October22 – 26 1981</u>

Eight years ago Ann Howard was Calgary's first Carmen and she returns with a burnished tone, a fire in the blood that admits no passage of time. There are other avenues to explore in a portrayal of Carmen, but on this level, which presents a gypsy blessed with passion, humour and love without the burden of caricature, there are only individual nuances to add.

Howard provides all the salient details.

November 1980: Work throughout this month on Massenet's *Don Quichotte*.

Keith and Ann in Nice

Don Quichotte is a comic opera in spite of the hero's sad death at the end. Ann played the role of La Belle Dulcinée, a much-admired beauty around whom the plot is set. It was a rarely performed opera, though it was done later by ENO with Alan Opie in the title role. A Hollywood film of the story (not an opera) was produced and Ann remembers auditioning for the role of Dulcinée. She didn't get it: the role was given to Sophia Loren.

1981

The year began by travelling to Groningen in Holland to rehearse *Boris Godounov* by Mussorgsky – Ann to sing the role of the Old Nurse and the Hostess. Performances in Utrecht followed. She returned to London to begin work on the role of Beppe in Mascagni's opera *L'amico Fritz* to be performed in New York.

A visit to the USA has particular memories for Ann. The opera was to be rehearsed and performed in New Jersey, but because there was great danger from Mafia activity in the area, the cast stayed in New York and were bussed out to New Jersey each day.

In March she was in Fort Worth to sing the role of Klytemnestra in *Elektra* by Richard Strauss.

Ann as Klytemnestra in Richard Strauss's opera 'Elektra' in fort worth, USA   Photo: Buddy Myers

Geoffrey Lockett, a personal friend of Ann's and an enthusiastic music-lover, owned a farm with a huge barn: Clonter Farm. He wanted to promote a concert there in May and asked Ann to sing at the first, promotional event. She remembers that the audience sat on bales of straw and that it was a great success. This became Clonter Opera which continues to this day. A feature was a competition for young singers and Ann was invited to be one of the judges in the following years.

Later in that same month she travelled to Glasgow to a Scottish Television show for Arthur Blake with Norman Bailey. These televised concerts were always a great pleasure for Ann. The music was light in character, often from pre-war shows. Blake became a personal friend and she often stayed in his grand Glasgow flat and enjoyed his hospitality.

In July she was with the opera festival in Buxton to sing in Cimerosa's opera *The Secret Marriage*.

*A scene from 'the Secret Marriage' by Cimerosa in the Buxton
production 1981 Ann in the role of Fidalma*

August 28th Commence work on *John Socman* for the BBC

September 7th – 121th Rehearsing *John Socman* in London.

September 14th – 17th Recording *John Socman* in Manchester

John Socman by George Lloyd was one of three operas commissioned for the 1951 Festival of Britain. The other two were *The Pilgrim's Progress* by Vaughan Williams and *Billy Budd* by Benjamin Britten. It was to be recorded by the BBC in Manchester, and conducted by Edward Downes – one of the several lesser-known operas that this conductor championed in Manchester. It was broadcast on February 7th 1982.

1982

In January Ann was in St Etienne, France to sing in Massenet's opera *Herodiade* and in the Spring rehearsals began for *The Grand Duchess of Geroldstein*.

Ann had sung the title role in La *Grande Duchesse* in two previous productions: in Santa Fe and with Welsh National Opera. This was to be a completely new production at Sadler's Wells – this time in English. The Sadler's Wells theatre had been taken over by Joseph Kariovitis who intended to put on a series of operettas, naming his company New Sadler's Wells Opera. This he succeeded in doing, though sadly the company eventually went bankrupt.

The Grand Duchess was to be a Victorian production. ('Not so pretty' – according to Ann). She remembers that she had to act with a shotgun at one point, and when it fired, the noise of the shot would come from the wings. On one occasion this shot failed to sound so Ann shouted 'bang!' to the great amusement of the audience.

A run of sometimes daily performances followed. After this marathon run, Ann's diary has many days where the entry simply reads '11-1', (a three hour morning session) or 2.30 (an afternoon session). Indeed, these entries appear many times in all her diaries. They refers to sessions with a repetiteur, most often Mary Nash, learning a new role, preparing concert songs or brushing up on her core repertoire. Then rehearsals began for *Ruddigore*, a Gilbert and Sullivan Savoy opera.

A production of *Ruddigore*, in which Ann played Mad Margaret, was to be televised for an American company. The cast included Keith Michell and Vincent Price. Ann greatly enjoyed working with Vincent Price. She said that he was a 'lovely, friendly man' and far nicer than the characters that he had assumed in his many horror films. It received several weeks of rehearsal followed by filming sessions which ended on July 3rd.

Gilbert and Sullivan's 'Ruddigore'. From left: Vincent Price, Ann (as Mad Margaret) and Keith Michell: a production for an American television station

In July Ann was doing a performance of *The Trojans* for a BBC Prom concert, and soon afterwards she was with English National Opera North for *Samson and Delilah*. The first night was on October 6th in Leeds.

Ann in the outrageous costume for Ligeti's opera 'Le Grand Macabre'

Left: A scene from Ligeti's opera 'Le Grand Macabre' with Dennis Wicks
Right: 'Le Grand Macabre' opened on December 2nd 1982 and caused a sensation in the press. Ann's local press in Kingston upon Thames (The Surrey Comet) dubbed her 'a pin-up for the Royal Navy' Photos: Clive Barda

The next few weeks found Ann continuing with the ENON tour of *Samson and Delilah* while also starting to rehearse György Ligeti's *Le Grand Macabre* for ENO, conducted by Elgar Howarth. Richard Jones was to give this work an imaginative production. It was to be a great success for Ann, not least of all because of the science fiction plot of the opera, the modern idiom of the music and her revealing costume with tights, corset and leathers. A whip completed the outfit.

October 18th Rehearsals commence for *Le Grand Macabre.*

Mireille. This opera by Charles Gounod was being staged by ENO at the express wish of one of their leading sopranos, Valerie Masterson. It was not very well received by the press and public, but Ann enjoyed the role of Taven, the Witch. Predictably this caused one journalist to write '. . . thank goodness there was a 'Taven' in the town.

A scene from the ENO production of 'Mireille' by Gounod. From the left: Valerie Masterson, Adrian Martin and Ann
Photo: Andrew March

1983

In January Ann was in Avignon to perform the role of Magdalena in Verdi's *Rigoletto*, thence to Toledo and Detroit for *Carmen* and on to New Orleans to sing in *Tristan and Isolde*. These recent engagements, which entailed a good deal of travelling and a lot of rehearsal, received very few performances – sometimes only one. Ann assured me that this was not unusual.

PRESS

Le Grand Macabre by György Ligeti

In the beautiful land of Breughelland, Nekrotzar,(Geoffrey Chard) the great macabre, rises Dracula-like from the grave to announce the imminent destruction of the world. He is heard with different degrees of incredulity by (the suitably named) Piet von Vat, an easy-going drunk; by Astradamus, (Denis Wicks) the court astrologer, and his whip-cracking, corseted high-booted wife Mescalena; (ANN HOWARD) by the ineffectual Prince Go-Go and his quarrelling ministers, and by the chief of the Secret Police, a coloratura soprano,(Marilyn Hill-Smith) dressed with her minions as sinister birds. The two lovers, (ballroom dancers) Miranda and Amando, (whose names were changed from Spermando and Clitoria – perhaps the only concession made to decency in this production) ignore Nekrotzar entirely. They find the grave . . . an ideal private nest for love-making, and spend the major part of the opera there, unseen and unscathed, emerging in the final scene to round the music with an ecstatic duet. Nekrotzar has failed: the world is intact; no one was hurt. He melts away: bur who was he? Death indeed? Or a false Messiah, a shabby jester playing a part.

Elijah Moshinsky's new production of Ligeti's totally crazy theatre-piece for the English National Opera is much less charming than the (original) Stockholm (production) and immensely more vivid.

Moshsinsky's designer Timothy O'Brien sets the centre of his Breughelland in the middle of a sinister overpass of the M4 Motorway, with crash-barriers, overhead signs and warning lights. Nekrotzar is suited, in long black leather, as Goebbels would have liked to appear if he's only been slimmer. The grave is not a grave at all, but a hearse with a bullet-hole through the windscreen slewed across the road. Astrodamus and Mescalina have their living room mid-motorway. The astrologer's telescope is mounted next to the roof of an Indian cinema and a rubber goods factory, on the gleaming red top of a number 27 bus.

Dominic Gill—THE FINANCIAL TIMES December 3 1982

Boos from above competed with cheers from the stalls at the final curtain of English National Opera's production of 'Le Grande Macabre' at the Coliseum last week. The opera's impish 60-year-old composer, Gyorgy Ligeti, leaped about the stage looking delighted. But as his work is designed to shock – he describes it as an anti-opera – I suppose he felt he'd achieved his aim.

I didn't actually feel the booing was entirely justified, for we had seen an undeniably interesting, often amusing, sometimes strikng performance, skilfully staged by producer Elijah Moshinsky, with brilliant designs and lighting by Timothy O'Brien and Nick Chelton. Not only that, but the entire cast had performed magnificently, and conductor Elgar Howarth led the orchestra with enormous skill.

One couple, dressed as for 'Come Dancing 'spent the whole evening making love in the back of a hearse. Whilst another, heavily into flagellation, had the wife in wasp-waisted corset, black stockings and boots – a virtuoso performance by ANN HOWARD – belabouring her husband with a whip. Venus appeared as a Marilyn Monroe look-alike, and Prince Go-Go, superbly played by counter tenor Kevin Smith in immaculate naval uniform, bore an uncomfortable resemblance to a member of the Royal Family.

David Fingleton—DAILY EXPRESS December 11 1982

ANN HOWARD splendid in fetishist dishabille. She is thoroughly vulgar and sexy, and she sings her music in character, proving that Ligeti's vocal writing can be an effective, exact and even touching vehicle of feeling.

Paul Griffiths—THE TIMES December 6 1982

CHAPTER 9

Character Roles

Work on Prokofiev's opera *The Gambler* with ENO began on March 29th. The role that Ann had was a true character role. Although she was still singing Carmen, she felt that it was now suitable for her to undertake more and more character roles. This role – Babulenka – (a rich old aunt who loved to gamble) was musically difficult, but gave her a wonderful opportunity to shout and 'throw her weight about' on stage.

Ann as Babulenka in the ENO production of Prokofiev's opera 'The Gambler' 1983

Photos: Zoe Dominic

PRESS

The Gambler by Sergei Prokofiev

ANN HOWARD's fruity grandmother (is) outstanding

Michael Kennedy—THE SUNDAY TELEGRAPH March 18 1990

ANN HOWARD is marvellously larger-than-life as the dragon of a Babushka

Edward Greenfield—THE GUARDIAN March 16 1990

. . . superb in stage presence and unquenchable vocal energy was the imperious Babushka of ANN HOWARD.

Anthony Payne—THE INDEPENDENT March 16 1990

Her (Sian Edwards) conducting begins cautiously, though very precisely, and then, from the shock arrival of the crazed old Grandmother – superbly played by ANN HOWARD – steadily gains in power, vivacity and rhythmic bite.

Robert Henderson—THE DAILY TELEGRAPH March 16 1990

As Babulenka (Babushka) ANN HOWARD is magnificent, her dottiness no less regal than before.

Max Loppert—THE FINANCIAL TIMES March 15 1990

A Return To Santa Fe

Orpheus in the Underworld was to be performed in French, but the character called Public Opinion spoke to the audience in English. However, Ann was given two arias from other Offenbach operas which she sang in French, and she also sang in French when singing with the chorus – reverting to speaking directly to the audience in English as a narrator at certain points in the opera. Ann enjoyed this production in Santa Fe as she had enjoyed the previous productions of *Carmen* and *The Grand Duchess*.

The opera season here always opened with a light opera or operetta. However, work was also beginning on *Arabella* by Richard Strauss – Ann to play Adelaide. With rehearsals complete, these two operas were performed on successive nights throughout the Santa Fe season: eleven performances of *Orpheus in the Underworld* and six of *Arabella*. It was two months of intensive work, but Keith and Katherine came out for some of the time and a great deal of socialising took place to make the whole experience very enjoyable.

Ann reminded me of how beautiful the place is – high up with clear air and with wonderful light, especially at night. The theatre itself being partially open, sometimes it used the mountain views as part of the scenery. It was a place originally founded by the native American Indians who still lived there. It was possible to buy their beautiful artefacts at that time, though subsequently these became prohibitively expensive

Rebecca received its world première in Leeds with ENON: Wilfred Josephs had created an opera out of the famous novel by Daphne du Maurier. Ann's part of Mrs Danvers was a rich character role which she very much enjoyed.

PRESS

Rebecca by Wilfred Josephs

Robert Cockroft writes of the revival: 'Peter Knapp and Ann Howard, both coping strongly with angular and often ungrateful musical lines, return to give respectively statuesque and chilling accounts of Maxim de Winter and Mrs Danvers.'

Robert Cockcroft also writes: 'Musically and dramatically the best performances come from Ann Howard as the sinister Mrs Danvers and from Peter Savidge as the incisive Favell. And the orchestra, in sterling form, delivers the busy score with great zest colour under Mr Lloyd-Jones's energetic direction.'

Michael Kennedy writes: 'Ann Howard's Mrs Danvers has become more menacing to good effect.'

Rusalka. Work on this modernized, full-scale production of Dvořák's opera *Rusalka* by the producer David Pountney for ENO (which would be eventually televised) continued for Ann until the first night on November 15th. Ann spoke warmly of her role as Jezibaba in this opera. She remembers the comic scene when she is making a witch's potion and she has to swing a cat above her head, bang it on the wall and fling it into the pot. 'It was all a lot of fun—and wonderful music of course—and a very, very good sing: rising phrases up to A flat. I very much enjoyed it.'

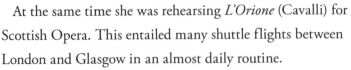

At the same time she was rehearsing *L'Orione* (Cavalli) for Scottish Opera. This entailed many shuttle flights between London and Glasgow in an almost daily routine.

Also at this time Ann was invited to sing in an 'off the wall' production of *Orpheus In The Underworld* for ENO. This included the whole cast wearing exaggerated Prince Charles ears. She was very disparaging about this. However, the production was cancelled because of an industrial strike.

PRESS

Rusalka by Anton Dvořák

Rusalka, (a wood nymph), passionately in love with a mortal prince, is made human by a witch with the proviso that she will be speechless and, if spurned by him, cannot return to her native condition. Inevitably, he rejects her in favour of a full-blooded, full-voiced princess!.. As the witch, ANN HOWARD contributed another of her baleful, black bombazine portrayals with accustomed style and a nice edging of wit

> Hilton Tims SURREY COMET June 20 1986

*Ann as the witch Jezibaba
in Dvořák's opera 'Rusalka'
ENO production 1984 Photo:
Clive Barda*

David Pountney's Victorian nursery production of Rusalka has returned to the English National Opera after a gap of 18 months. New to the cast (is) ANN HOWARD, who has a whale of a time as the witch-governess..

Paul Griffiths—THE TIMES November 17 1984

No longer an operatic oddity, no longer just the frame for 'O silver moon', Rusalka is revealed in this production as a masterly piece of theatre by a major European composer (Dvorak) in his final surge of creativity . . . Among singers new to the cast this season, ANN HOWARD as Jezibaba (the witch transformed into a stern mother or governess) trod, like the fine artist that she is, exactly on the line between irony and caricature. Her 'spell' turned out, in Rodney Blumer's clever translation, some splendid borrowing from the witches in *Macbeth*.

OPERA MAGAZINE December 1984

1984

In January of this year, in Rouen, Ann sang her very last performance as Carmen, feeling that she now preferred to sing character roles (the wickeder the better). She was then into rehearsals for both *War and Peace* by Prokofiev and *Rusalka* by Dvořák.

In France: Ann with Gilbert Py in one of her last appearances as Dalila in Saint-Säens's
opera 'Samson and Dalila'

War and Peace was one of the operas that ENO took on tour in the USA. There were performances in Austen, Texas and at the Metropolitan Opera in New York. On returning to London she had roles in *Irmelin* by Delius (for BBC radio) and *L'Orione* by Cavalli for Scottish Opera which Ann described as a 'sweet opera'. In September she travelled to Santiago in Chile to sing *Samson and Delilah*.

Chile, at this time, was a politically unstable country under the rule of General Pinochet. Ann was travelling alone and felt somewhat nervous about this. She boarded the aircraft and started to stow her bags in the locker. While her back was briefly turned a thief took her bag containing her money, valuables and passport. This meant that she would have to enter the country with no money or passport – a worrying prospect. Of course she immediately reported it to the crew and a search was mounted. She suffered a number of hours of anxiety before this bag mysteriously turned up on a seat in another part of the aircraft. Clearly the thief realised that everyone would be searched and his crime discovered, but Ann remembers the incident as being truly terrifying.

October 2nd: *Samson and Delila* first night in Santiago. Ann remembers this as a beautiful production. It was also to be her last performance as Delilah. She was fifty, and still well able to sing the role, but felt that she shouldn't be doing glamorous roles any more. 'I don't want to be seen as one of those people who are seen to be doing roles that they shouldn't really be doing.' She saw her future doing character and comic roles which she greatly enjoyed.

1985

To Santa Fe once more (Ann sang there for five seasons altogether).

The two operas in rehearsal in Santa Fe were *Orpheus in the Underworld* which Ann had sung last year and John Eaton's *The Tempest*. Ann remembers that *The Tempest* was a Jazz opera and she had to sing in a Jazz group in a 'pop' style for which she received special instruction. ('That was fun'.) She even had to sing while having a fit of hiccups. 'God, this was the most difficult piece I have ever been in. I played Caliban the monster. It was incredibly difficult music – virtually un-singable'. However, she received very good reviews.

Ann as Caliban in John Eaton's opera version of William Shakespeare's play 'The Tempest. Santa Fe Opera 1985

PRESS

The Tempest by John Eaton

Not until 50 minutes into Act 1 did the audience sit up, enlivened by the spectacle on stage. In fact operagoers nearly leaped into the aisles to dance when a funky jazz beat brought mezzo soprano Ann Howard, looking like Queen Kong as Caliban, shimmying and shaking on stage. After so much effort to find melody, the audience finally found some energy. So it goes, with the wicked getting the best parts –' Eaton's use in reference to Caliban permits Howard uninhibited mugging. She dives into the beat without hesitation.'

Allen Young—THE ROCKY MOUNTAIN NEWS August 4 1985

A trio of alto sax, electric guitar and electric bass represents the bestial Calian (Mezzo, Ann Howard) and his drunken revels with Trinculo and Stephano are celebrated with some exquisitely low-down jazz-rock that closes the first act in a brilliant theatrical burst.'

Michael Walsh—TIME August 19 1985

The scene-stealing favourite, however, was Ann Howard, who sported a Maurice Sendakesque monkey suit as a wild and wooly Caliban-in-reverse-drag who had to scat-sing the blues.'

Martin Bernheimer—THE LOS ANGELES TIMES August 1985

Ann appeared in the title role of Katya Kabanova by Leoŝ Janáček in the 1985 ENO production.

Ann as Katya in the 1985 ENO production of Janácek's opera 'Katya Kabanova'

Photo: Clive Barda

THE MIKADO

1986

The very successful Jonathan Miller production of Gilbert and Sullivan's *The Mikado* with the comic actor Eric Idle at the Coliseum had received its first run during the time that Ann was doing *Il trovatore*. Now she was to play Katisha in the second run. It was set in a luxury hotel foyer in the 1930s and took its cue from the British fad for all things Japanese, without *looking* Japanese. Ann asked if her head dress was to be Japanese and the reply was 'You don't want to have knitting needles in your hair do you'?

Ann was (and still is) a great fan of Eric Idle. They appeared together in a Royal Command Performance in which they sang 'Always look on the bright side of life' from the Monty Python film, *The Life of Brian*. Idle wrote a radio play with a singing and acting part especially for Ann.

The first night was on October 18 and was received with rapturous reviews and has remained in the ENO repertoire ever since, with frequent revivals.

Ann as Katisha with Eric Idle and Richard Angas in the ENO production by Jonathan Miller of Gilbert and Sullivan's opera 'The Mikado' Photos: Catherine Ashmore

IL TROVATORE

Ann appeared in Verdi's opera *Il trovatore* twice in her career, singing the role of Acuzena: once for Welsh National Opera in 1964 and then for English National Opera immediately before she joined the cast of *The Mikado* in 1986

Ann in the role of Acuzena in Verdi's opera 'Il trovatore' Photo: Catherine Ashmore

PRESS

Il trovatore by Verdi

To all people who are irritated, frustrated or plainly infuriated by the story of 'Il Trovatore' – and hardly anyone really understands it, however much they pretend – let me offer two simple words of advice. Forget it. Concentrate instead on Verdi's music and the emotions and dramatic situations become immediately clear and what happens to whom, or even worse, what is supposed to have happened before the opera even starts, really doesn't matter.

It was the last of the Welsh National Opera Company's five operas at the Odeon Theatre, Llandudno this week and last night's production was a powerful one. ANN HOWARD, singing the Gipsy role of Acuzena for the first time, was well cast and gave an outstanding vocal performance besides projecting herself excellently into the part.

Neil Barker—LIVERPOOL DAILY POST August 22 1964

1987

Ann's diary for this year is not very informative. There are hastily written entries to indicate many learning and rehearsal sessions but few details. She points out that at this time rehearsal periods were far longer than when she first joined Sadler's Wells Opera at the beginning of her career. Two or three weeks was all that was spent on production rehearsals then. Now, seven or more weeks were scheduled.

THE PLUMBER'S GIFT

Ann's memories of David Blake's opera *The Plumber's Gift* were that it was an unusual modern work which received a brilliant production by Richard Jones. She played Mrs Worthing – a seaside landlady – a comic role. The opera was staged on a circular platform that only had one door for entries and exits. Inevitably this door got stuck on one occasion and the players had to squeeze on through the scenery.

Scenes from the ENO world première of 'The Plumber's Gift' by David Blake. Ann with Neil Howlett

PRESS

The Plumber's Gift by David Blake

Nicholas Kenyon gave the opera a great deal of harsh criticism, but of Ann he observed:

'Ann Howard's Dame Edna-esque seaside landlady is a splendid comic creation: for her, and for the conductor Lionel Friend, one has admiration and sympathy.'

Nicholas Kenyon—OBSERVER—

May 28 1989

Top Left: A scene from 'The Plumber's gift'

Lower Left: Ann as Mrs Worthing – a seaside landlady

CANDIDE

1988

Ann took the role of the Old Lady in Leonard Bernstein's *Candide*. 'I loved *Candide* – I loved all the music; it was a lovely part for me – 'I'm easily assimilated' was my big number – and I played the castanets – it was such fun. The biggest thrill of my career happened when Leonard Bernstein came to rehearsals. I actually sat and talked to him – knee to knee – and he told me how to sing with a Jewish accent.'

Scenes from Leonard Bernstein's opera 'Candide'. Scottish Opera production 1988
Next page top: Ann with Marilyn Hill Smith singing 'Glitter and be gay'
Next page below: Ann, Mark Tinkler and Leon Greene singing 'What's the use'   Photos: Eric Thorburn

THE MARRIAGE OF FIGARO

1989

The first half of the year found Ann singing regular performances of *The Mikado* and *The Plumber's Gift*, then, in August, she started work on the role of Marcellina in *The Marriage of Figaro*. This was the only Mozart role that she undertook, feeling that Mozart was not her style. The critics did not agree with her and gave her good reviews.

PRESS

The Marriage of Figaro by Wolfgang Amadeus Mozart

The translation into English was fresh and witty, allowing the cast to show some fine comic abilities. ANN HOWARD in particular shone as Marcellina – this lady has wonderfully expressive eyes and she uses them to full advantage here, playing up to, and feeding from, David Gwynne's Bartolo.

GLASGOW HERALD October 1989

A scene from ENO's pantomime 'Cinderella or the Glass Subsidy' which was performed as part of a gala evening in honour of Lord Goodman, ENO's long-serving Chairman. December 21st 1986. Ann played the Good Fairy Jenny Lee, (the former Labour arts minister and champion of the arts.) Photo: Catherine Ashmore

Ann's diary is full of travel arrangements during this last period her career: airport times, taxis and railway sleepers. As well as moving about in Scotland, she also returned a number of times to London.

On November 20 she was with ENO for a rehearsal on *The Gambler*. At the end of the diary for 1989 is a list of engagements for the future including *Peter Grimes, The Gambler, Gipsy Baron* and *Die Fledermaus*. Clearly the next few years were going to be as busy as ever.

INTO THE WOODS

"Into the Woods"

Cinderella's
stepmother
Act I.

Sue Blane '90

*Costume design for Ann's role as Cinderella's
wicked step mother in Sondheim's West end show
'Into The Woods'*

1990

During the learning and rehearsal period for
Peter Grimes, Ann was also working on *Into
the Woods*, a musical by Stephen Sondheim for
performance in London's West End.

It featured various fairy stories. She was to play
Cinderella's stepmother.('Not a sympathetic role.')
She remembers a grisly scene where she had to cut
off the toes of one of her daughters.

To make this look realistic she was coached by
Imelda Staunton's husband, Jim Carter who later
became well-known for his role as the butler in
the television series *Downton Abbey*.

The show was produced by Richard Jones.
Sondheim attended some of the rehearsals. The
show included two opera singers of whom Ann
was one. The other was Mark Tinkler with whom
Ann had previously sung in *Candide* .

The other performers were actor/singers from
the world of West End musicals.

PREVIEWS FROM 14th SEPTEMBER
OPENS 25th SEPTEMBER

A new musical

Music and Lyrics by   Book by
STEPHEN SONDHEIM   JAMES LAPINE

Starring

JULIA McKENZIE

IMELDA STAUNTON   PATSY ROWLANDS

CLIVE CARTER

with

EUNICE GAYSON   ANN HOWARD   IAN BARTHOLOMEW
JACQUELINE DANKWORTH   MARK TINKLER   JOHN ROGAN

and

NICHOLAS PARSONS

Directed by
RICHARD JONES

Set by   Costumes by   Choreography by
RICHARD HUDSON   SUE BLANE   ANTHONY VAN LAAST

Orchestrations by   Musical Director   Musical Supervisor
JONATHAN TUNICK   PETER STANGER   MARTIN KOCH

Lighting by   Magic by   Sound by
PAT COLLINS   ROVANI   ANDREW BRYCE

Producer
DAVID MIRVISH

PHOENIX THEATRE
Charing Cross Road, London, WC2

For the next four to five months Ann performed eight times a week in the show *Into the Woods* . In her whole career she only did two shows. The first one was *Wild Grows the Heather* at the very beginning, and now this Sondheim show. It was a tough assignment, but as always, Ann enjoyed it.

PETER GRIMES

1991

Ann took the role of 'Auntie' in Britten's *Peter Grimes*. She loved the opera. 'It was a wonderful, wonderful piece'. Later she was to sing it at the Met. in New York, at the Bavarian State Opera in Vienna, and also for the Welsh National Opera. In fact it became the last opera that she sang before retirement.

PRESS

Peter Grimes by Benjamin Britten

English National Opera production. April 1991

The individual set against the community, Peter Grimes against the Borough: there you have the theme of Benjamin Britten's first operatic masterpiece, and never has that stark opposition been so sharply realised as in Tim Albery's new production for English National Opera.

. . . the two mezzo roles, Anne Collins as the widow Sedley and ANN HOWARD as Auntie, the landlady of The Boar, convey an almost Wagnerian weight.

Edward Greenfield—THE GUARDIAN April 19 1991

Most British productions of recent years have stressed Grimes's links with the past and presented it as an isolated piece of English *verismo.* Now the opera is back with the English National Opera – whose parent company, Sadler's Wells Opera, first performed it – and for the first time, it emerges as a harrowing psycho-drama, laden with a collective post-war angst, which places the work in a wider European context . . . . (The cast, including) ANN HOWARD's bosomy Auntie . . . all contribute to one of the most musically and theatrically riveting ENO evenings I can ever recall.

Hugh Canning—SUNDAY TIMES April 21 1991

A new Peter Grimes must have posed a particularly weighty responsibility for English National Opera. Britten's masterpiece is part of its heritage, an historic landmark in its company's CV when , as Sadler's Wells Opera, it staged the world premier in 1945. The new production is ENO's first since then . . . and duly has been honourably discharged . . . . The vignette roles which Britten drew so tellingly are marvellously realised in ANN HOWARD's Auntie, Anne Collin's Mrs. Sedley and Jonathan Summers Balstrode.

Hilton Tims SURREY COMET April 26 1991

. . . as with all Britten's work, the secondary roles are strongly developed. They are brought to vivid life in this production by ANN HOWARD, Rosa Mannion and Claire Daniels as Auntie Ia and the nieces.

Marese Murphy—GLASGOW HERALD April 27 1991

THE ROYAL VARIETY SHOW

Ann meets Her Majesty the Queen after The Royal Variety Show 1991

Ann met the Queen after the Royal Variety Show. She also remembers enjoying the company of Les Dawson whom she describes as very charming as well as very funny. (I loved him – such a sweet man). He told her that he was going to be in pantomime at the Richmond Theatre and Ann promised to be there. Very sadly he died before the pantomime opened.

Her performance in a sketch with Eric Idle began with her singing a spoof version of 'One Fine Day' and ended with them both singing 'Always look on the bright side of life.' It was hilarious. A filmed extract has been repeated a number of times on television.

1992

At the beginning of this year Ann was in the middle of a run of Johann Strauss's *Die Fledermaus*. She had the role of Prince Orlovsky for which she was given a military costume made of heavy white wool, over which she had to drape an equally heavy coat. She hated this, especially as it made her look enormous. She was also asked to wear a sword, but this she wisely refused to do – not wishing to injure either herself or Lesley Garrett (singing the part of Adele) with whom she had to perform a dance sequence.

By early April Ann was in Leeds to rehearse the role of the Hostess in Moussorgsky's opera *Boris Godounov*. Ann had first sung this role in 1981. The title role was to be sung by John Tomlinson who went on to enjoy great success with it. It was a six-week long rehearsal period.

Ann commented many times about the increasing length of rehearsal periods for opera productions. This was largely due to the great emphasis now being placed on the production rather than the music – a fact that was reflected in the press reviews which wrote extensively about the staging and production and made little comment about the singing.

1993

Ann had worked with Mark Tinkler in *Candide* and *Into the Woods*. She described him as tall and handsome – a fine singer – and had very much enjoyed their partnership. Now Tinkler wanted to start his own opera company, a project which Ann was happy to support. A concert was arranged to promote the idea. Camberwell Pocket Opera was formed, eventually becoming Pocket Opera.

With her schedule of opera appearances now a little easier, Ann started to receive pupils at her home. Much of the summer of this year was to be spent in this teaching. In March she was asked to sit on an adjudicating panel at the Royal Northern College of Music to judge and assess young musicians.

Ann worked on two operas by Richard Strauss this year: *Elektra* and *Salome*. These were for BBC Proms. Some visits to Munich followed.

Peter Jonas, who had been an administrator at ENO, was now the Intendant of the Staatsoper in Munich. He arranged for the ENO production of *Peter Grimes* to be performed there. Performances took place in December and January 1994.

1994

The year began in Munich at the Bavarian State Opera with the ENO production of Britten's *Peter Grimes*. Back in London soon afterwards there was a long rehearsal period of the work in preparation for a televised performance from the London Coliseum. The first night was on May 20th, and special televised performances commenced in June.

HMS PINAFORE

In early July Ann flew to New York to rehearse the role of Little Buttercup in the Gilbert and Sullivan opera *H.M.S. Pinafore*. This production was one of a number of Savoy operas sponsored by a university in New York with a campus in Purchase. Many British singers were brought over to perform. Ann returned in subsequent years to sing *The Sorcerer* and *Iolanthe*.

Gilbert and Sullivan's opera 'HMS Pinafore' in New York.

Ann as Little Buttercup with Richard Suart (Captain Corcoran)

As Ann had enjoyed a great success in Purchase with *HMS Pinafore*, she was invited to sing with the Metropolitan Opera in New York. This was to be a completely different production of *Peter Grimes*. The leading role of Ellen Orford was played by Renée Fleming. Rehearsals continued in New York until the first night on December 12th.

1995

Back in London Ann started to work with the repetiteur Phillip Thomas on two works: *Sancta Susanna*, a one-act opera by Paul Hindemith for a BBC Prom performance and *Street Scene* by Kurt Weill for performance in Portugal. *Sancta Susanna* was given a concert performance in the Barbican in January and later, a Prom in the Royal Albert Hall. Her memories of this are not particularly happy – but she loved *Street Scene*. It is more of a musical than an opera, with a lot of dialogue which had to be spoken with an American accent. Ann had the role of Emma Jones – a character role of an old crone; (yes, another 'bitch' role). 'A fine piece of music. I loved it – a fabulous role – the numbers in it are simply wonderful and it had an impressive production using the whole stage to display a panorama of Broadway'. The cast was international; indeed, the plot is set in a boarding house where people from four different countries live.

It was performed in Lisbon, Portugal, conducted by John Mauceri with whom Ann had previously sung *Candide* in Scotland – a happy collaboration. There were four performances in May and June. In July, Ann returned to Purchase to sing in a Gilbert and Sullivan opera with the University of New York. She was also busy teaching.

In December of this year Ann went to Turin in Italy to sing *Street Scene*. She returned just before Christmas to receive some alarming news from Keith. He had received a letter informing him that Ann had been diagnosed with breast cancer. The festive season was clouded with worry over this. She was operated on in the New Year and happily made an excellent recovery. Speaking about it today she implied that it was only a small matter – that she always knew that she would return to full health; however, for a person who had enjoyed perfect health throughout her career, it must have been a great shock.

1996

A new opera by Peter Maxwell Davies, *The Doctor of Myddfai*, was produced in this year by Welsh National Opera. This two-act opera, based on the Welsh myth of The Lady of the Lake had a libretto by David Pountney (who also produced it) and was conducted by Richard Armstrong. It received a long period of rehearsal and a number of performances but was not a success in spite of some rather wonderful Welsh male-voice choir singing. Ann had the role of one of three officials; she has few memories apart from a hilarious occasion when all three collided on stage resulting in helpless laughter.

In September Ann went again to Purchase, this time to sing The Fairy Queen in *Iolanthe* and in November she was in the new run of *The Mikado* for ENO at the London Coliseum.

1997/8

Ann is now sixty and into the last few years of her operatic career. Her days of singing Carmen – of which she sang over 250 performances – and the Grand Duchess and Delilah are behind her, but a succession of character roles come her way and there are still new challenges. She also has a busy teaching practice; she wanted to pass on Modesti's excellent method of voice production which had served her so well.

After this last run of *Peter Grimes* in Munich, Ann was invited to sing in the Vienna State Opera production of this opera. It was again a completely different production – very modern – with some quirky ideas. She remembers that Peter Grimes had his leg attached to a boat that he had to drag around the stage. She sang in three performances.

1999

In this year Ann would become sixty-five and would embark on the last big project of her career: *Peter Grimes* for Welsh National Opera. This was to receive a completely new production by the German producer

Peter Stein. Stein announced that this would be the 'definitive production' (a claim that somewhat offended the British press.) There was a seven-week rehearsal period in Cardiff so Ann and Keith (who had retired by this time) took a flat near the rehearsal venue.

Ann did not enjoy a happy relationship with Stein, possibly because she refused to audition for the role – having sung it in London, Munich, at the Met in New York and with the Vienna State Opera. Stein never called her by her name, only referring to her as 'Auntie' – a fact that Ann thought was insulting.

Ann found the long weeks of rehearsal very stressful. She was also beginning to suffer a lot of back pain. This was to develop into the painful arthritis that has dogged her life since. It must have been easy for her to have lost patience with this tremendous emphasis on production. In the early days of her career an opera would receive only two or three weeks, but now a massive, and sometimes wasteful amount of money would be spent on production. In the course of this production expensive scenery was constructed, only to be jettisoned. Ann was fitted for an extravagant pair of hand-made boots which, again, were not finally used in the performances. Furthermore, the sets failed to fit into the different theatres on tour, so numerous extra rehearsals were made necessary.

The opera opened in Cardiff to less-than enthusiastic reviews. Perhaps the press had its own agenda. A tour followed.

Above: Welsh National Opera's production of Britten's opera 'Peter Grimes' with Charlotte Page and Nicola Howard (1st and 2nd nieces), Janice Watson (Ellen) and Ann (Auntie) Photo: Bill Cooper

Below: A scene from the Welsh National Opera's production od Britten's opera 'Peter Grimes' with (from the left) Peter Bronder (Boles), peter Savidge (Ned Keene) and Ann as Auntie.   Photo: Bill Cooper

It was during this tour that Ann thought long and hard about her career – a career that had spanned 50 years. Touring is tough and she had been round the country many times with a number of different operas. She began to feel that she had done everything that she wanted to in opera – had sung many wonderful roles, and performed all over the world. She certainly never wanted to continue so long that people noticed that she was 'past it'.

PRESS

Peter Grimes by Benjamin Britten

Welsh National Opera's production of Britten's 'Peter Grimes' has been eagerly anticipated: directed by Peter Stein and conducted by WNO music director Carlo Ritzi. Both tackling one of the great 20th-century operas for the first time . . . . . Naturally, there's no hint of cosy British parochialism in Stein's staging, and Ritzi conducts as if it were one of Verdi's angrier late operas – lots of sound and fury, with the famous WNO chorus singing fit to bust . . . . There were neat performances from Peter Bronder as the Methodist fanatic, ANN HOWARD as the Landlady, Neil Jenkins as the parson, Iain Goosey as John (the boy) and Janice Watson as Ellen and Donald Maxwell (Balstrode).

Rodney Miles—THE TIMES March 27 1999

Of the vignettes, ANN HOWARD's Auntie, Peter Bronder's Boles and Ann Ewing's Hobson rate special mention, though all are excellent.

Stephen Walsh—THE INDEPENDENT February 22 1999

In Cardiff, Peter Stein's new production of 'Peter Grimes' is much as he said it would be in these pages two weeks ago: in a word, 'conventional' . . . . there were stalwart contributions from ANN HOWARD (Auntie), Andrew Greenan (Swallow), Peter Bronder (Bob Boles), Alan Ewing (Hobson) and, especially, Susan Gorton as a fearsome, rabble-rousing Mrs Sedley. A good Grimes, but not, perhaps, the revelation we were led to expect.

I seem to be alone in admiring Peter Stein's staging of Britten's 'Peter Grimes' for Welsh National Opera at the New Theatre, Cardiff (and later on tour). If one thought one had become inured through familiarity to the dramatic and emotional impact of this work, this was a performance to take one back to raw first impressions. The storm nearly blew us out of our seats, the Borough inhabitant's manhunt cries of "Peter Grimes!" froze the blood – what a chorus – and their persecution of Ellen Orford in Act 2 was almost as vicious . . . . ANN HOWARD's Auntie (was) well sung and characterised.

Michael Kennedy—SUNDAY TELEGRAPH February 21 1999

At this time her voice was still in good shape, but she knew that voices lose their beauty and charm as the singer ages. It was easy for her to mention a number of prominent opera singers who had sung into their old age and rather spoiled their reputation. Perhaps too, the sheer hard work of keeping a voice in tip-top condition was something that she no longer wished to do. Also there was the travelling and being away from her home and family. Finally there was the increasing back pain which made standing for long rehearsals quite agonising.

It was when the WNO *Peter Grimes* tour visited Liverpool that her mind was fully made up to retire. She was staying in a hotel which was close to the Aintree race track. On the evening after the Grand National a great many revellers descended on the hotel and kept her awake into the wee small hours. It was the last straw. She was in no way bitter about this decision. She genuinely felt that there was nothing left that she wanted to do. She had had enormous pleasure and fulfilment from her years of singing and had earned a comfortable living. She had met and worked with many charming people; indeed she said that opera people were the very nicest theatre people and she got on well with just about everyone. (She was not so complimentary about pantomime people, who, she said, had their own act within the performance and had little time for other actors.)

She started to think back over the years. She commented that, after the first couple of years, she never had to audition to get a role. She was always invited. This is quite unusual. Nowadays even prominent singers are asked to audition. Furthermore, she was never out of work.

I then made a quick summary of how she progressed from one part of her life to another. There was always someone 'in charge' of her life. To start with it was her mother who organised it for her to work in London after leaving school. Ann simply 'did as she was told' and seemed fairly happy to do so. Soon she had met Keith who planned her first moves into the profession. The wonderful scholarship that she had to go to Paris and study with Modesti was offered to her without her needing to apply, and again, Keith was there to help and guide her. On returning to London, she was not ambitious and would have remained a member of the Covent Garden company singing minor roles for many years, but Keith had grander ideas. He arranged for her to audition for Sadler's Wells where she would undertake principal roles. Once she began to get established her career schedule was taken over by her agents. Unlike many people in show business she never had to 'network' or curry favour with promoters. The work just seemed to come to her: very fortunate, but also an indication that she was well-known for doing a good job. Also, because she managed to get along well with the people that she worked with, she was frequently asked back to do more performances. 'Awkward' singers, (and they are legendary), often find themselves out of work.

CHAPTER 10

The Opera Houses

I asked Ann to recall the various opera houses in which she had worked. She immediately said that the Met in New York was her all-time favourite. It was very well run and administered with every possible facility. There were always people to see to makeup and wigs (not always the case in other theatres) and she commented especially on the doorkeeper who, in spite of seeing hundreds of people, immediately got to know Ann, greeting her by name almost from the first day of working there. 'Very much the nicest place that I worked in.'

Munich was also a favourite. There was an international staff and singers from all over the world. Ann remembers a lot of good laughs which sweeten the hard business of getting an opera on stage.

There were fewer laughs in the Vienna State Opera where demands were made and expected to be carried out. She noted that both the Munich and Vienna opera houses had been rebuilt after the destructive bombing in World War Two.

In many theatres the beauty and glamour of the front-of-house was often in stark contrast to the facilities in the dressing rooms. Toilets were often shared between several dressing rooms and there was usually a depressing tattiness in the decor. She loved working in Avignon as the audience was so enthusiastic, but the opera house was no luxury. Bordeaux's house also needed much improvement in the years that Ann sang there.

Of course she loved Covent Garden. She had loved it when she first joined the Royal Opera as a member of the chorus and always looked forward to working there when she returned later as a principal singer. At the London Coliseum she remembers that the two major dressing rooms had a lavatory between them with a door for each room. This led to hilarious situations. If this loo was occupied one had to run some distance down the corridor.

The old Sadler's Wells theatre was notoriously uncomfortable though Ann has lovely memories of it. The new Sadler's Wells is very modern and almost over regulated (in Ann's opinion.).

These 'Houses' are almost a second home to busy opera singers and Ann is not alone in having many memories of them. The physical facilities are very important, but so is the degree of help, and the quality of the overall atmosphere. A friendly and appreciative House can make the experience of working there particularly enjoyable, and arguably enhance the quality of the performances.

CHAPTER 11

The Wall Of Death

Any live performance is a 'wall of death' insofar as unexpected things can go wrong and cause a nerve-wracking situation. All performers have their horror stories which, although terrifying at the time, make hilarious stories. Ann is no exception. Her worst nightmares concerned doors.

One of her frequently performed roles was that of the Witch in *Hansel and Gretel*. This witch is finally dispatched by being pushed into the oven where the gingerbread is being cooked. Clearly this is a vital point in the story – so what can be done if the oven door will not open? This indeed happened on one memorable occasion. There was much pulling and pushing, and eventually, with a destructive lurch of breaking scenery the door opened and the crisis was over.

Ann sang in many performances of *Carmen*, one of the most bizarre being in a bull ring at the end of a real bullfight in Mexico. She remembers awaiting the entry of Don José – the music pausing for what seemed like an eternity. Where was he? He eventually appeared and later told the story of how, because he was dressed in a shabby costume, some over-zealous security guards detained him for questioning. No doubt this took time as nobody spoke the same language.

The Plumber's Gift was staged on a small circular set with only one door for entrances and exits. This invited a problem, and sure enough this door got badly stuck during one performance. What was to be done? While the music continued members of the cast wrestled with the recalcitrant door, to no avail. Finally people had to squeeze uncomfortably through gaps in the scenery and the proscenium arch.

In each of these moments the whole story of the opera would have been ruined if a quick solution had not been found. Did the audience notice the near panic on stage? Possibly not as professional actors and singers are marvellously good at improvising a solution. Even so, the wear and tear on the nerves must have been considerable.

Nervous tension is 'par for the course' in opera. Apart from the ever-present possibility of things going wrong with either the music or the production there is the story being told – a story that is so often tragic. Operatic characters experience dramatic situations which have to be realistically acted out: death, betrayal, bereavement, murder are all to be graphically portrayed. It is hard not to let the emotion from these scenes spill over into normal life. Ann described to me how laughter is an excellent release from this tension; the darker the tragedy the louder the laughter. She even said that she enjoyed a bit of tap dancing in the wings. Perhaps the audience – who might well be in tears at the sadness of the story and the convincing performances on stage – feel that these shenanigans and laughter are inappropriate, but perhaps they are very necessary for the performer. One great exception to this was when Ann sang in Wagner's *Tristan and Isolde*, an opera that always brought genuine tears to her eyes.

CHAPTER 12

The Producer

To any opera singer the producer is a person of significance.

Ann's first experience of this was with the completely new production of *Carmen* for ENO with John Copley. She enjoyed a very close collaboration with Copley who built the whole production around her. He had the overall concept of Carmen as a believable woman, full of life and energy. Equally believable was the fight scene with the cigarette girls in Act 1. This was carefully choreographed to look convincing – a feature the critics particularly admired. This perfectly matched Ann's idea of the role. Copley took great pains over every detail including costume and make-up; (Ann had to colour her whole body in brown skin make-up.) The production was an enormous success and many performances followed.

When ENO produced Wagner's *Ring* (the famous 'English Ring') there was a trio of important people who combined to get this great work on stage: producers Glen Byam Shaw and John Blatchley and conductor Reginald Goodall. Ann remembers that they all worked well together. Byam Shaw was a theatre producer of long-standing eminence having worked at the National Theatre with such great actors as Sir Ralph Richardson and Sir Laurence Olivier. The younger, energetic Blatchley ran up and down the aisles of the theatre to convey communications between the other two.

'I loved working with Colin Graham' Ann said. Graham, unlike Copley, preferred to work in smaller-scale operas – chamber operas that were more like plays. Richard Rodney Bennett's *The Mines of Sulphur* was one such opera which Ann enjoyed very much. With Richard Jones she had a rather livelier relationship.

Richard Jones had many exciting ideas about opera production. One idea that was never performed was in a production of *Die Fledermaus.* Ann had the role of Prince Orlovsky who has a famous aria to sing: 'Chacun a son goût'. Jones thought it would be amusing to have a gorilla come on stage during this aria – and climb up the curtain.

In the same opera (in which she had a heavy white woollen military costume complete with cloak) Jones suggested at the dress rehearsal that she carry a sword. Ann pointed out that this would be quite dangerous in the dancing scene. Ann admired Jones's fertile imagination, but had to put a restraining hand on it at times. In *The Plumber's Gift* Ann was Mrs Worthing, a seaside landlady and Jones had the idea that she should be in the foyer, hoovering the carpet before the start of the performance. Ann categorically refused as her theatrical instincts told her that stage people should not appear in the front-of-house. Happily these disagreements didn't sour their good working relationship.

It was sad then that Ann did not enjoy a happy relationship with the producer in the last opera that she performed: *Peter Grimes* with WNO, produced by Peter Stein. There were probably many reasons for this, but from the start Stein appeared less than friendly. Matters came to a head over a steep flight of steps on stage that Ann had to

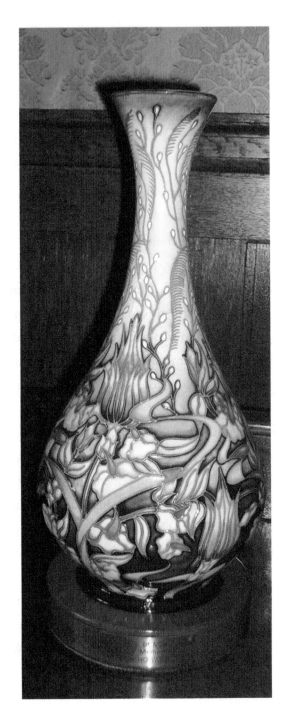

negotiate. She requested a hand rail which Stein did not wish to see. She refused to use the steps without it – and a rail was put in place,to the considerable relief of many other members of the cast – but it didn't improve relations between them.

But this was not typical of Ann's experience. She had had 50 years of working on stage – busy, wonderful years in which she worked with hundreds of people and been both happy and successful.

Our conversations rarely had a sour note and even today she still has friendly contact with many former colleagues and fellow singers. She is left with her memories, which I was privileged to share.

Previous page: The Worshipful Company of Musicians presented Ann with their special Charles Sandley Memorial prize to honour her years of eminence on the opera stage. The very beautiful Moorcroft vase was Ann's own choice and now has pride of place in her home.

CONCLUSIONS

What are my final thoughts as our Conversations draw to an end?

Certainly I have been blown away by the story of so much sustained success; also astonished at the sheer hard work of an opera singer. As I list the roles that she undertook, some of which had to be sung in English one moment and in the original French, German or Italian the next, and contemplate that each of these had to be committed to memory along with the different production requirements, I am amazed.

She herself is very modest about her achievements and always emphasises that she loved every moment.

It was a physically tough job, with a great deal of travelling and many long learning sessions and rehearsals. I indeed wonder if any aspiring young singer who reads this book can face such a challenge.

I have also shared some of her private life and her memories of home, marriage and motherhood, and felt the warmth of her personality.

In spite of a glittering career that often took her away from home, she has had, and is still having – a full and happy life.

Ann and Keith's daughter Katherine grew up and presented Ann with a grand daughter: Jasmin Ann Millicent

Ann in 2012 with her beloved dog Charlie

LIST OF STAGE ROLES

FIRST PERFORMANCES	Role
1965/6	
Gipsy Baron (J. Strauss)	Gipsy Queen
La bohème (Puccini)	Musette
Oedipus Rex (Stravinsky)	Jocasta
L'heure Espagnole (Ravel)	Concepcion
Hansel and Gretel (Humperdinck)	Witch
The Valkyrie (Wagner)	Fricka
Samson and Delilah (Saint Saëns)	Delilah
The Trojans (Berlioz)	Cassandra
The Mines of Sulphur (Bennett)	Leda
1967	
Iolanthe (Gilbert and Sullivan)	Fairy Queen
The Rake's Progress (Stravinsky)	Baba the Turk
1968	
Ariadne auf Naxos (Richard Strauss)	Prima donna/Ariadne
1969/70	
Orfeo (Monteverdi)	Two minor roles
Bluebeard (Offenbach)	Boulotte
Carmen (Bizet)	Carmen
Kiss me Kate (Cole Porter)	Lilly Vanessi
1971	
Lohengrin (Wagner)	Ortrud
1972	
Aïda (Verdi)	Amneris

1973

Tristan and Isolde (Wagner)   Brangäne

The Rhinegold (Wagner)   Fricka

La traviata (Verdi)   Flora Bervoix

The Grand Duchess of Gerolstein (Offenbach)   The Duchess

1974

Arden Must Die (Alexander Goehr)   Mrs Arden

1976

La Belle Hélène (Offenbach)   Hélène

1977

The Italian girl in Algiers (Rossini)   Isabella

1978

The Force of Destiny (Verdi)   Preziosilla

The Consul (Menotti)   The Secretary

Don Carlos (Verdi)   Princess Eboli

1980

Die Fledermaus (J. Strauss)   Prince Orlovsky

Don Quichotte (Massenet)   La Belle Dulcinee

1981

Rigoletto (Verdi)   Maddelena

L'amico Fritz (Mascagni)   Beppe, a gipsy

Boris Godounov (Mussorgsky)   Old Nurse and the Hostess

Elektra (Richard Strauss)   Klytemnestra

Il trovatore (Verdi)   Azucena

The Secret Marriage (Cimarosa)   Fidalma

1982

Herodiade (Massenet)   Herodiade

Ruddigore (Gilbert and Sullivan)   Mad Margaret

Le Grande Macabre (Ligeti)	Mescalina
1983	
The Gambler (Prokofiev)	Babulenka
Orpheus in the Underworld (Offenbach)	Public Opinion
Arabella (Richard Strauss)	Adelaide
Rebecca (Wilfred Josephs)	Mrs Danvers
Mireille (Gounod)	Taven, a witch
1984	
War and Peace (Prokofiev)	Princess Marya
Rusalka (Dvorák)	Jezibaba the Witch
L'Orione	
1985	
The Tempest (John Eaton)	Caliban
Katya Kabanova (Janácek)	Katya
1986	
The Mikado(Gilbert and Sullivan)	Katisha
1987	
The Plumber's Gift (David Blake)	Mrs Worthing
1988	
Candide (Bernstein)	The Old Lady
1989	
The Marriage of Figaro (Mozart)	Marcellina
1990	
Peter Grimes (Britten)	Auntie
Into the Woods (Sondheim)	An opera singer
1994	
HMS Pinafore (Gilbert and Sullivan)	Little Buttercup
1995	

Street Scene (Kurt Weill)	Emma Jones
1996	
The Doctor of Myddfai (Maxwell Davies)	A Secretary

This list does not include operas that Ann performed for radio. Edward Downes promoted many, often obscure, operas which were broadcast from Manchester by the BBC.

CAREER HISTORY

ABBREVIATIONS

ENO	English National Opera	Oed.Rx.	Oedipus Rex
ENON	English National Opera North	L'Heure	L'heure Espagnole
LC	London Coliseum	Ariad.Nx.	Ariadne auf Naxos
RFH	Royal Festival Hall	Troj.	The Trojans
RAH	Royal Albert Hall	G&S	Gilbert and Sullivan
ROH	Royal Opera House	M of Fig.	The Marriage of Figaro
ROCG	Royal Opera Covent Garden	P. Gr.	Peter Grimes
SWO	Sadler's Wells Opera	In. Woods	Into The Woods
SW	Sadler's Wells Theatre	HMS Pin.	HMS. Pinnafore
SO	Scottish Opera	Il trov.	Il trovatore
STV	Scottish Television	Gip. Bar.	Gipsy Baron
NYCO	New York City Opera	Mi. Sul.	Mines of Sulphur
LPO	London Phiharmonic Orchestra	C. Ory	Count Ory
Rhine.	The Rhinegold	Arden.	Arden Must Die
Valk.	The Valkyrie	TV	Television
Twil.	Twilight of the Gods	Prog.	Programme
H&G	Hansel and Gretel	Perf.(s)	Performance(s)
It. Girl	Italian Girl in Algiers	Reh.(s)	Rehearsal(s)
Sams&Del.	Samson and Delilah	mat.	Matinee
Trist.& Isol.	Tristan and Isolde	SF	Santa Fe (New Mexico, USA)
Die Fled.	Die Fledermaus	NY	New York
Bel.Hel.	La Belle Hélène	Edin.	Edinburgh

1956

Ann was discovered by Jack Waller, giving her her first professional engagement : Wild Grows The Heather .

In the following years Ann worked in Pantomime until she joined the chorus of The Royal Opera, Covent Garden

1962

Still in the chorus of ROCG at the beginning of this year.

October 25	To Paris with Keith to study with Modesti
Oct. 29	First lesson with Modesti Remained in Paris studying for 6 months

1963

February 23	Returned to London to rejoin the ROCG, Now a minor principal to sing The Dama, (Macbeth) and Kate Pinkerton, (Madama Butterfly)
November 27	Successful audition for Sadler's Wells Opera

1964

Ann (now aged 30) joined Sadler's Wells Opera, continuing for a while to sing with ROCG

April 16	First BBC broadcast/Home Service
May 26/27/30	Gipsy Baron: Leeds (first role with SWO)

Started regular concerts with Mary Illing

June 1/4/6	Gipsy Baron: Oxford SWO
June 9	Gip. Bar. 1st night/ London SW
June 10/12/13/17/19/20/23/24/27	
	Gip. Bar. SWO at SW
July 5	Gip.Bar. Reh. For TV
July 10/17	Mary Illing concert: Folkestone
August 4	Hansel and Gretel Rehs. SWO
Aug. 6/7/10/11	Rehs. Valkyrie SWO
Aug. 12	To Cardiff Reh. Il trovatore WNO
Aug. 17/18/19	Il trov. Rehs. WNO
Aug. 21	Il trov. 1st night Cardiff WNO
Aug. 22/26/27/28/29	Ring Rehs. SWO
Aug. 31	Valkyrie: General Reh.
Sept. 1	Rhinegold: General Reh. and Twil. (Norn) Reh.
Sept. 3	Rhinegold: Perf.
Sept. 5	Valkyrie: Perf.
Sept. 7 – 10	Ring Perfs. and Twil.. Rehs
Sept. 13	Mary Illing concert: Bexhill
Sept. 14	Twil.: Reh.
Sept. 15/16	Hansel and Gretel Reh.
Sept. 17	Twil.. General Reh.
Sept. 19	Twil.. 1st night

Sept. 21/22/26	Ring cycle:		Jan. 18/19/25/26/27/29	
October 1	Mines of Sulphur: Learning			Min. Sul. Rehs. SWO
Oct. 2/6	Hansel and Gretel: Reh. SWO		Jan. 21/28	H&G Perf. SWO
Oct. 7	H&G: record for EMI, Abbey Rd.		February 1 – 6	Min.Sul. Rehs SWO
	(H&G was recorded before the stage run)		Feb. 8 – 15	C .Ory Rehs. SwO
Oct. 8	Mines of Sulphur: Learning SWO		Feb. 16	H&G Perf. ENO
Oct 11	H&G EMI recording		Feb. 17 – 20	Min. Sul. Rehs. SWO
Oct 21 – 24	H&G Rehs. SWO		March 1	Min. Sul. Reh. SWO
Oct. 26/27	Min. Sul./Gip. Bar. Rehs. SWO		March 22	C. Ory General Reh. ENO
Oct. 28	Min.Sul Reh. SWO		March 23	C. Ory 1st night SWO
November 4/5	H&G Bradford SWO		March 26	Min. Sul. Reh.
Nov. 14	H&G matinee SWO		March 26	Min.Sul. Manchester
Nov. 17/21	H&G Aberdeen ENO		April 17	Concert: with Tom Hammond
Nov. 25/26	H&G Newcastle (Mat. on 26) SWO		April 18	Concert: Tom Hammond Blackpool
Nov. 27	Min. Sul. Reh. London SWO		April 29/May 7	Iolanthe: Perfs.
December 1/5	H&G Liverpool SWO			Begin SWO European tour
Dec. 9/10	H&G Birmingham SWO		May 11/12/13	To Zagreb: Iolanthe at Croation
Dec. 19	H&G 1st night SWO LC			National Theatre
			May 14	Return to London
1965			May 15	To Paris to visit Modesti
			May 16/17	Min.Sul. Rehs. SWO
Jan. 4	Min. Sul./Count Ory Rehs SWO			Continuing SWO European tour
Jan. 5/6	Count Ory Reh. SWO		May 18	To Amsterdam
Jan. 7	H&G Perf. SWO		May 21	Iolanthe: Amsterdam
Jan. 11	Concert: Mary Illing		May 26/27/29	Gip. Bar. Amsterdam
Jan. 13	H&G Perf. SWO		June 2/4	Iolanthe: Vienna
Jan. 14	Min. Sul./C. Ory Rehs. SWO		June 6	To Bratislava/Prague
Jan. 16	BBC: Grand Hotel		June 8	Iolanthe: Prague

June 11/12/16/18	Gip. Bar. Prague	Jan. 23/25/26/27	Oedipus Rex: Rehs. SWO
July 6/8/10	Orfeo: Cambridge	Jan. 2/25	BBC: *Memories of Sadler's Wells*
July 14/17	Iolanthe:	Jan. 29/30/31	H&G Filming for TV SWO
August 27	Concert with Mary Illing: Folkestone	Feb. 1/2	Oed.Rx. Reh. SWO
September 6/7/8	Valkyrie: Rehs. ROCG	Feb. 2/3	Sams.&Del. Reh. SWO
Sept. 11	Reh. with Solti ROCG	Feb. 4	Die Fled. SWO
Sept. 13/14/18/20/21/13		Feb. 7/9	H&G Norwich SWO
	Valk. Rehs. ROCG	Feb. 17	Sams.&Del. Hull SWO
Sept. 14/15/16/24	Orfeo: Rehs. SWO	Feb. 27	Oed.Rx/L'Heure Espagnol Rehs.
Sept. 21	To Glasgow	Feb. 28	Ernani: 1st night SWO
Sept. 22	Sams.&Del. SWO Glasgow	March 1/2/6 – 27	Oed.Rx Rehs. Fittings SWO
Sept. 29	Sams&Del. SWO Aberdeen	March 11	Dancing Years EMI recording
Oct. 6	Sams.&Del. SWO Edinburgh	March 2/16/23/28/30	Iolanthe: Rehs. SWO
Oct. 13	Sams.&Del. SWO Bradford	March 29	Oed.Rx. 1st night SWO
Oct. 15	Waltz Dream: Camden theatre/	April 3	Iolanthe Reh. SWO
	Recording	April 4	Iolanthe 1st night ENO
Oct. 20	Sams.&Del. SWO Blackpool	April 5/7/11/13/14	L'heure. Rehs. SWO
Oct. 31/Nov. 1/2/3	Sams.&Del. Rehs	April 8/19/21	Oed.Rx. Perfs. SWO
November 9	Sams.&Del. 1st night SWO	April 12/14/18	Iolanthe: Perfs. SWO
Nov. 12/16/23/26	Sams.&Del. SWO	April 27	Recording EMI
Dec. 22	Hansel and Gretel: 1st night SWO	May 3/9/19	Iolanthe: Perf. SWO
Dec. 26/27/28/31	H&G SWO	May 6	BBC: Gala Night At The Opera
		May 15/16	Oed.Rx/ L'heure. Rehs SWO
1967		May 23	Oed.Rx./L'heure Perf. Oxford
		May 31	Oed.Rx./L'heure. Birmingham
Jan. 2/5/7	H&G SWO	June 13	BBC: Vienna City Of Dreams
Jan. 10/12/14/16/21	H&G Stratford SWO	August 7/9	Sams.&Del. Rehs. SWO
Jan. 21	Ernani: Reh. SWO	Aug. 10	Orpheus in the Underworld: 1st night

Aug. 11	Rake's Progress: Reh. SWO	Jan. 22/23/25	Ariad. Nax. Rehs. SWO
Aug. 26	Sams.&Del. 1st night SWO	Jan 26/27	BBC: The Dancing Years
Aug. 29	Sams.&Del. SWO	Feb. 3	BBC: Perchance To Dream
September 4/7	Sams.&Del. Newcastle SW O	Feb. 5	To Leeds for press conference
Sept. 13/15	Sams.&Del. Bradford SWO	Feb. 6/23/28/29	Ariad.Nax. Rehs. SWO
Sept. 29	Sams.&Del. SWO	March ½	Ariad.Nax. Rehs. SWO
October 7/11	Sams.&Del. SWO	March 15	Ariad.Nax. 1st night SWO LC
Oct. 21	Concert: Mary Illing Scarborough	March 19/21/28	Ariad.Nax. SWO LC
Oct. 31/Nov. 4/14	Sams.&Del. SWO Glasgow	March 21	Ariad.Nax. BBC recording
Nov. 18	BBC: Ivor Novello broadcast	March 23	Force of Destiny: Reh. Guildford
Nov. 25	Rake's Progress: Reh. Liverpool SWO	March 30	Concert: Swansea
Nov. 26	Rake's Progress: Liverpool SWO	April 5	Ariad.Nx. SWO LC
Nov. 27	H&G Rehs. begin	April 8/12	Sams.&Del. SWO Leeds
Nov. 30	Concert: Stockton-on-Tees	April 14	Concert: Scarborough
December 2	Sams.&Del. Perf. SWO	April 1925/26	Rusalka ROCG
Dec. 4/5	The Mikado: TV recording	April 29	Ariad.Nx. Reh
Dec. 12/16/19	H&G SWO	April 30	Rusalka ROCG
Dec. 21	Rigoletto	May 2	Ariad.Nx. SWO Newcastle
Dec. 27	Sams.&Del. Stratford SWO	May 6	Rusalka: Reh. For BBC
		May 7/8	Rusalka: BBC
1968		May 9	Ariad.Nx. SWO Liverpool
		May 10/11	BBC recording
1968:	SWO moves to the London Coliseum	May 16	Ariad.Nx. SWO Nottingham
Jan. 1/2/4/5	Ariadne auf Naxos: Rehs. SWO	May 18	Concert; Swansea
Jan. 6	Sams.&Del. SWO Stratford	May 23	Ariad.Nx. SWO Bristol
Jan. 13/19	H&G Perfs. SWO LC	May 30	Ariad.Nx. SWO Bournemouth

June 13	Iolanthe at Sadler's Wells theatre
Aug. 21	Ann and Keith's daughter born
October 5	Concert: Scarborough
Oct. 8/9	Sams.&Del. Rehs. SWO
Oct. 12	Concert: Scarborough
Oct. 17 – 21	Sams.&Del. Rehs. Manchester
Oct. 22/25	Sams.&Del. SWO Manchester
Nov. 15	Sams.&Del. 1st night SWO LC
Nov. 18/21	Sams.&Del. SWO LC
Nov. 18/21/22/23	Cendrillon: BBC recording
Nov. 26/29	Sams.&Del. SWO LC
Nov. 27	BBC interview at LC
December 1	BBC: Grand Hotel
Dec. 4/13	Sams.&Del. SWO LC
Dec. 18	Force of Destiny: 1st night

1969

January 7	H&G Perf. SWO
Jan. 8/24	Orfeo: Reh. SWO
Feb. 25/28	Sams&Del SWO Newcastle
March 3/5/6/8/10/13 – 15	
	Orfeo: Rehs.
March 6/7	The Trojans: Rehs. ROCG
March 20	Orpheo: 1st night SWO LC
March 24/25/27/28	The Trojans Rehs. ROCG
March 26/Apr. 1	Orfeo SWO LC

April 4	Concert: Calder Valley
April 8/9	Troj. Reh. Manchester
	Reh. with the Halle Orchestra
April 10	Troj. Perf. Manchester/Halle
April 14 – May 2	Troj. Rehs. SO
	Rehs. In London and Glasgow
May 3	Troj. 1st night Glasgow SO
May 7/8	Aïda: Rehs.
May 10/14/19/24	Troj. Perfs. SO
June 24/26/28/30	Ullyses/ Mavra: Reh.BBC
June 25/27	Troj. SO
June 28	BBC: Ullyses: Rehs./ Maida Vale
	At 10.30am. and 1.30 pm. Also:
	BBC: Grand Hotel Reh. RFH 4.15pm.
June 29	BBC: Ullyses: 3 Rehs./ Maida Vale
June 30	BBC; Ullyses: 2 Rehs. Also:
	Grand Hotel broadcast
July 1	BBC: Ulyses: 2 Rehs./ Maida Vale
July 7/9/21/23	Troj. Reh

At this time Ann was covering the role of Cassandra in the Trojans for ROCG but performing it with SO

July 9	Mavra: Learning
July 8/10/11/22/24/25	Bluebeard: SWO
July 22	Rake's Progress: Reh. SWO
August 9/10/14	Mavra: Rehs. BBC Prom
Aug. 15	BBC: Prom/Stravinsky/Mavra
Aug.18/20/21	Troj. Reh

Aug. 21	Semele: BBC: Prom Reh.
Aug. 22	Semele: BBC Prom Perf.
Aug. 27	Bluebeard: Reh. SWO
Sept. 2/3/6/8/9/13	Bluebeard: Reh.SWO
Sept. 16 – 19	Bluebeard: Rehs. SWO
Sept. 22/23	Bluebeard: Liverpool SWO
Sept. 25	Rake's Progress: 1st night SWO
Sept. 29/30	Bluebeard: Bradford SWO
Oct. 1	Rake's Progress: SWO
Oct. 2	Bluebeard: Reh. SWO
Oct. 4	Bluebeard: 1st night SWO
Oct. 8/11	Bluebeard: Sunderland SWO
Oct. 13	Concert: Rake's Progress: Aberdeen
Oct. 14	Rake's Progress: Edinburgh SWO
Oct. 15/18	Bluebeard; Edinburgh SWO
Oct. 21	Rake's Progress: Aberdeen SWO
Oct. 22/25	Bluebeard: Aberdeen SWO
Oct. 30/Nov1/4	Bluebeard: Glasgow SWO
Oct. 31/Nov 6	Rake's Progress: Glasgow SWO
Nov. 11/13/17/22/26/28	
	Bluebeard: SWO LC
Nov. 20/25	Rake's Progress: SWO LC
Dec. 1	Rake's Progress: SWO LC
Dec. 4/8/13/26/27	Bluebeard: SWO LC
Dec. 11/17	Rake's Progress: SWO LC
Dec. 12	BBC: Gypsy Princess: 3 Rehs.

1970

January 29	Valk. 1st night SWO LC
Feb.2/6/10/14/16/21	Valk. SWO LC
Feb. 17/18/19/20/23	BBC: Gypsy Baron
March 2/6	Oedipus Rex: Rehs. SO
March 7/8	Oed.Rx. SO at Bute Hall
March 10	Oberon: Reh. Carmen: Reh. SWO
March 12/13	Carmen: Reh. SWO
March 17 – 20/26/29/31	
	Oberon: Rehs. SWO
April 1	Oberon: RFH SWO
May 6	Carmen 1st night SWO LC
May 8/11/14/20/23/26/30	
	Carmen: SWO LC
June 10/11	Beethoven 9th Symph. Rehs .for
	Bath Festival
July 13	Carmen: Reh. SWO
July 14/15/16	Veronique: BBC Reh. /Record
August 4	Carmen: 1st night new run SWO LC
Aug. 4/12/15/22/27	Carmen: SWO LC
Aug. 11	BBC: Birmingham:
	David Hughes show
Sept. 10 – 13	The Kiss: BBC. Manchester
Sept. 15/18/26/29	Carmen: SWO LC
Oct 10/Nov. 3	Semele: Reh. SWO
Oct. 22/23	Concert: Scottish TV Glasgow
Nov. 30	BBC: Eric Robinson show/record:
Dec. 24	Kiss Me Kate: 1st night SWO LC

This show continued until Jan. 23 1971

1971

Jan. 3	BBC: Sunday Night at the Coliseum
Jan. 29/30	La Fille de Madame Argot
Feb. 3	Carmen: 1st night new run SWO LC
Feb. 5	BBC: Friday Night Is Music Night
Feb. 13/16/18	Carmen SWO LC
March 9/12/18	Carmen: SWO LC
March 17	Valk. 1st night SWO LC
March 20	Valk. SWO LC
March 21 – 25	To Paris and Dusseldorf
	Return to London
March 27	Valk. SWO LC
March 31	Carmen: SWO LC
April 2	Valk. SWO LC
April 11	To Oxford, USA via Miami
April 12	Carmen: Rehs. Start Oxford USA
April 14/15	Carmen: Rehs. Oxford USA
April 16/18	Carmen: Perfs. Oxford USA
	Return to London
April 22/28	Carmen: SWO LC
April 24/30	Valk. SWO LC
May 3/12	Carmen: SWO LC
May 8/14/22/28	Valk. SWO LC
May 17	Carmen: Leeds SWO
May 26/31	Carmen: Newcastle SWO
June 5	Valk. SWO LC
June 30	To Vienna

July 1	Audition in Vienna
July 17	Kiss Me Kate: 1st night SWO LC
August 12	Lohengrin: 1st night SWO LC
Aug. 16/20/24	Lohengrin SWO LC
Sept. 2/10/17/22/30	Lohengrin SWO LC
Sept. 8	Carmen: SWO LC
Sept. 24 – 27	Die Fledermaus: Filming for TV
October 4/7/9/14	BBC: Osud: Rehs./Record
Oct. 5/12/15	Carmen: SWO LC
Oct. 16	BBC: Osud: Reh./Record
Oct. 20/22	Lohengrin SWO LC
Oct. 26/29	Iolanthe: SWO LC
Nov. 4/5	Scottish TV Show Glasgow
Nov. 8/9/22	Aida: Rehs. SWO
December 5	Concert: Guildford

1972

February 5	Twil.: 1st Night SWO LC
Feb. 9/12/16	Twil. SWO LC
Feb. 17	Carmen: 1st night new run
Feb. 21	BBC: Reh. LPO
Feb. 27	BBC: Concert: LPO Barking Town Hall
March 1	Rhinngold: 1st night SWO LC
March 4/14/18/21/25	Rhine. SWO LC
March 7/9	Carmen: SWO LC
March 11	Twil.. SWO LC
April 1/8/15/22/29	Twil. SWO LC

April 3/7	Carmen: Bristol SWO
April 12/17/21	Carmen: Manchester SWO
April 26	Carmen: Edinburgh SWO
May 1/5	Carmen: Edinburgh SWO
May 6/13/17/27	Twil.. SWO
May 10/15	Carmen: Leeds SWO
May 19/20/21	BBC: The Nose Manchester
May 24/29	Carmen: Oxford SWO
June 2	Carmen: SWO LC
June 3	Twil. SWO LC
July 11/12	Scottish TV show
July 29	Carmen: 1st night new run
	SWO LC
August 1/4/10/12/15/18	
	Carmen: SWO LC
Aug. 20	TV. Show
Aug. 23	Il trovatore 1st night SWO LC
Sept. 1	Aïda: Rehs. Begin in Toronto
Sept. 19/223/29	Aïda: 1st night Toronto

Keith and Katherine join Ann in Toronto

Oct. 1/5/11/14	Aïda: Toronto
Oct. 15	To New York
Oct. 27	Carmen: New York
Nov. 5/11	Carmen: New York
	Return to London
Nov. 17/18/19	To Los Angeles

Nov. 23	Broadcast with Tom Cassidy
Nov. 26	Return to London
Dec. 2	Carmen: mat. SWO LC

1973

Jan. 17	To Nancy to Reh. Sams & Del.
Jan 26/28	Sams&Del. Nancy
Jan. 29	Return to London
Feb. 3/7/12/15/19/20/22	
	Tristan Rehs. SWO
Feb. 13	Rhine. Reh. SWO
Feb. 21	BBC: Agamemnon Reh.
Feb. 26/28	Rhine. Rehs SWO
March 2/3/4	BBC: Agamemnon/ Manchester
March 6	Rhine. Reh. SWO
March 11	BBC TV: Good Old Days/Leeds
March 15	Tris&Isol: Reh. Tom Gligeroff SO
March 2/28/30	Rhine. Perfs. SWO LC
April 3/6	Aïda ROCG
April 5/11	Start of SWO tour: Rhine. Leeds
April 28	Trist.&Isol. Glasgow SO
May 2/5/11	Trist.&Isol. Glasgow SO
May 6	BBC: Music For Your Pleasure
May 9	Rhinegold: Liverpool
May 15	Valk. Reh. ROCG
May 17/19	Trist.&Isol. Newcastle SO
May 22/23/24	Trist.&Isol Rehs. Glasgow SO

May 26	Trist.&Isol. Edinburgh BBC Relay
May 29/June 1	Trist.&Isol. Edinburgh SO
May 31	Rhine. Manchester SWO
June 6	Rhine. Manchester SWO
	End of SWO Tour
June 7/9	Trist.&Isol. Aberdeen SO
July 2/3	STV: The Melody Lingers On/Edin.
July 31	Rhine. SWO LC
Aug. 4	Valk. SWO LC
Aug. 7/8/9	The Melody Lingers On/STV/Edin.
Aug. 14/18	Valk. SWO LC
Aug 16	Rhine. SWO LC
Aug. 27/28	Rehs.
Aug. 29	Trist.&Isol. London SO
Sept. 3	Mines of Sulphur: Reh. SWO
Sept. 12	Katya Kabanova 1st night SWO LC
Sept. 20/21/22/23	Min.Sul Rehs. SWO
Sept. 27	Min.Sul. 1st night SWO LC
Oct. 1	Trist.&Isol. Leeds SO
Oct. 5	Session on Carmen and Traviata with
	John Barker
Oct. 12	Min.Sul. last Perf. SWO LC
Oc.t 21	To San Diego USA to Reh. Carmen
Oct. 29/31/Nov. 2/4	Carmen in San Diego
Nov. 12/13	Carmen: Phoenix, Arizona
Nov. 14	Return to London
Nov. 20	Almost daily to Dec 10 BBC:Traviata

Dec. 18	BBC: Music For Your Pleasure with Barry
	Knight

1974

In this year, SWO was re-named English National Opera

Jan 14	Bluebeard: Reh. ENO
Jan 18/21/23/25	Arden Must Die Reh. ENO
	(Learning with John Barker)
Jan 27	To Calgary to Reh. Carmen
Feb. 7//9	Carmen; Perfs. Calgary
Feb. 10	Return to London
Feb. 13/16/22/25	War and Peace: Reh. ENO
Feb. 14/28	Carmen: ENO
Feb 19	BBC. Invitation To Music
Feb. 26/27	Arden Must Die Reh. ENO
March 1/13/16/18	Arden. Rehs. ENO
March 12/15/20/27/30	
	Carmen: ENO LC
March 22	Rhine. Reh. ENO
March 25/26/28/29	Arden. Rehs. ENO
April 1 – 13	Arden. Rehs. ENO
April 14/15	BBC: Armide: Reh.
April 15/16	Arden: Final Rehs. ENO
April 17/18/19	Arden. Perfs. ENO

April 20	BBC: Armide Test/Record	June 2/3	Rhinegold: Manchester
April 24/29	Ring: Rehs. ENO	June 5/13	Grand Duchess: Llandudno
May 6	Rhine. Perf. ENO LC	June 14	Concert: Ebbw Vale Vale
May 7	Valk. Perf. ENO LC	June 26	Grand Duchess: Southsea
June 27	To Santa Fe	July 17 – Aug. 24	Santa Fe to sing Carmen
July 19	Grand Duchess: 1st night SF	Sept. 3/6/12	Grand Duchess: Cardiff
July 24/27	Grand Duchess: SF	October 17	Grand Duchess: Swansea
August 1	L'Egisto: 1st night SF	October 22/24	Grand Duchess: Birmingham
Aug. 6/10/15/24	Grand Duchess: SF	November 8	Grand Duchess: Oxford
Aug. 9/21	L'Egisto SF	Nov. 9/10	Carmen Reh: Rouen
Aug. 25	Return to London	Nov. 16/18	Carmen: Rouen
Sept. 4 – 9	Learning with Mary Nash	Nov. 19/21	Grand Duchess: Manchester
Continuing to work with Mary Nash to end of Sept.		Nov. 27	Mahler 2nd Symphony: Birmingham

Oct. 3	To New York/Milwaukee Reh. Aïda	**1976**	
Oct. 10/12	Aïda in Milwaukee		
Oct. 20	To Edmonton to Reh. Carmen	January 7	Valkyrie Reh: ENO
Oct. 31	Carmen in Edmonton	Jan. 13	Rhinegold Reh: ENO
Nov. 2/4	Carmen in Edmonton	Jan. 19/20	Rhine./Valk: Perf. ENO LC
	Return to London	Jan. 25	Baltimore Reh. Grand Duchess
Nov. 6	Carmen ENO LC	February 12/14/16	Grand Duchess: Baltimore
Nov. 24	To Rouen to Reh. Sams&Del.	Feb. 17	Return to London
Nov. 29/Dec. 1	Sams&Del. Rouen	April 2	To Fort Worth, Texas
Dec. 8	Carmen; Hemel Hempstead Choral Soc.	April 9/11	Aïda: Fort Worth
		April 14	To Liège
1975		April 22/24/27/29	Sams&Del. In Liège
		May 1/2/7/9	Sams&Del. In Liège
May 27/31	Grand Duchess: Swansea	May 11	Belle Hèlène Reh. London

May 11	Carmen Reh: (afternoon): London
May 12/13	Belle Helene Reh: for Sunderland
July 5	Hansel & Gretel Reh: BBC TV
August 4	Come Sunday: Southern Television
August 29	Concert: Edinburgh/Arthur Blake/TV
September 4	Grand Duchess: Reh: Toronto
Sept. 24	Grand Duchess: 1st night Toronto
Sept 27/30	Grand Duchess: Toronto
October 2/5/6	Grand Duchess: Toronto
Oct 7	Return to London
Oct. 14	Fly back to Toronto
Oct. 16	Grand Duchess: Toronto
Oct. 17	To Ottowa
Oct. 21/23	Grand Duchess: Ottowa. Fly home
November 24/25	Carmen: Reh: Fort Worth
December 3/5/9	Carmen: Perfs. Fort Worth
Dec. 10	Fly to London
Dec. 12/13	Tales of Hoffman: Reh.
Dec. 14	Tales of Hoffman: concert RAH
Dec. 17	Bel.Hel.: ENO London LC
	(Rehearsals during earlier tour)
December 21	Bel.Hel.: ENO LC

1977

January 1/7	Bel.Hel.: ENO London LC
February 1	Aïda: Reh. Bordeaux
Feb. 11/13/15	Aïda: Bordeaux

Feb. 16 – 18	Flew home for two days
Feb. 20	Aïda: Bordeaux
March 20	To Avignon
March 25/27	Sams&Del. In Avignon
March 28	Carmen Reh. New York
April 2/12/27	Carmen: NYCO
May	Italian girl in Algiers: Learning
June 24	BBC: Reh.
June 25	BBC concert: RAH
September 1	To New York
Sept. 8/17	Carmen: New York
October 2	To Rouen
Oct. 7/9	Sams&Del. Rouen
Oct. 30	To Baltimore
Nov. 1/2/3	It. Girl: Reh.
Nov. 17/19/21	It. Gir:l Perfs. Baltimore
Nov. 23	Return to London
Nov. 27	To Avignon
Dec. 4/7/9/11	Carmen: Avignon

1978

January	Rehearsing throughout the month
Jan. 18	BBC at Maida Vale
February 12	Concert: Guildford
	(This concert was with Robert Bickerstaff, a former pupil of Modesti)
Feb. 26	To New York

March 5	Carmen: NYCO	October 18/25/29	Carmen: New York
March 9/18/24/29	Carmen: New York	November 30	To Los Angeles
March 30	Return to London	Dec. 3/10	Carmen: NYCO Los Angeles
March 31	Carmen: Reh. ENO	Dec. 11	Return to London
April 12	Carmen: 1st night ENO LC	Dec. 12	Hansel & Gretel Reh. For ENON
April 12/15/18/22/25	Carmen: ENO LC	Dec. 14	To Leeds
April 20	BBC Interview	Dec. 14	Hansel & Gretel: Reh. ENON

(To choose 2 records and sing a song)

April 28	BBC Reh. 2.30pm – 5.30pm.	*1979*	
April 28	Carmen: ENO LC		
April 29	BBC concert: RFH	January 3	Hansel & Gretel: 1st night ENON Leeds
May 13	To Guadalajara, Mexico	Jan. 4/8/10/12	Rehearsals at LC
May 18/20	Carmen: Monterrey	January 5/9/11/13	Hansel & Gretel: Leeds
May 21	Return to London	Jan. 14	To Toledo, Mass. Carmen: Reh.
May 25	Music Club of London: Interview	Jan 21	Carmen: Toledo
July 7	To Vichy	Jan 27	Carmen: Dayton
July 9/11	Carmen: Vichy	Jan 28	Return to London
July 12	Return to London	Jan 29	Carmen: Reh. ENO
July 16	The Force of Destiny: Reh. ENO	Jan 30	Carmen: Dress Reh.
August 12	The Consul: 1st night ENO LC	Jan 31	Hansel & Gretel: Hull ENON
August 18/23/25/29	The Consul ENO LC	February 1	Carmen: 1st night ENO London
September 1/6	The Consul LC	Feb. 2	Dancing Years: voice-over: Elstree
Sept. 3	ENO concert: RFH	Feb. 6/10/13/16/20/22/27	
Sept. 10	To New York		Carmen: ENO LC
Sept 16/24	Carmen: (matinee) NYCO	Feb. 7/9	H&G: Ashton-under Lyme ENON
Sept. 25 – Oct 11	Don Carlos: Baltimore	Feb. 15	H&G: Stratford
Sept. 12	Don Carlos: 1st night Baltimore	Feb. 14/21	Rheingold: Reh)in German)
Sept. 14/16	Don Carlos: Baltimore	Feb. 28	Valkyrie/Rheingold: Reh.

March 2	Carmen: ENO LC	January 3	Hansel & Gretel: 1st night ENON Leeds
March 14	Rheingold: Reh. in Naples	Jan. 4/8/10/12	Rehearsals at LC
March 18	Return to London	January 5/9/11/13	Hansel & Gretel: Leeds
March 19/22	Carmen: Liverpool	Jan. 14	To Toledo, Mass. Carmen: Reh.
March 23	Travel back to Naples	Jan 21	Carmen: Toledo
April 3	Rheingold: 1st night Naples	Jan 27	Carmen: Dayton
April 6/8/10/12	Rheingold: Naples	Jan 28	Return to London
April 20/21	Carmen: Montreal	Jan 29	Carmen: Reh. ENO
April 22	Return to London	Jan 30	Carmen: Dress Reh.
April 23	Carmen: Reh. For concert perf.	Jan 31	Hansel & Gretel: Hull ENON
April 24	BBC sessions: afternoon / evening	February 1	Carmen: 1st night ENO London
April 30	Carmen: Washington NYCO	Feb. 2	Dancing Years: voice-over: Elstree
September 1/6	The Consul LC	Feb. 6/10/13/16/20/22/27	
Sept. 3	ENO concert: RFH		Carmen: ENO LC
Sept. 10	To New York	Feb. 7/9	H&G: Ashton-under Lyme ENON
Sept 16/24	Carmen: (matinee) NYCO	Feb. 15	H&G: Stratford
Sept. 25 – Oct 11	Don Carlos: Baltimore	Feb. 14/21	Rheingold: Reh)in German)
Sept. 12	Don Carlos: 1st night Baltimore	Feb. 28	Valkyrie/Rheingold: Reh.
Sept. 14/16	Don Carlos: Baltimore	March 2	Carmen: ENO LC
October 18/25/29	Carmen: New York	March 14	Rheingold: Reh. in Naples
November 30	To Los Angeles	March 18	Return to London
Dec. 3/10	Carmen: NYCO Los Angeles	March 19/22	Carmen: Liverpool
Dec. 11	Return to London	March 23	Travel back to Naples
Dec. 12	Hansel & Gretel Reh. For ENON	April 3	Rheingold: 1st night Naples
Dec. 14	To Leeds	April 6/8/10/12	Rheingold: Naples
Dec. 14	Hansel & Gretel: Reh. ENON	April 20/21	Carmen: Montreal
		April 22	Return to London
1979		April 23	Carmen: Reh. For concert perf.

April 24	BBC sessions: afternoon / evening
April 30	Carmen: Washington NYCO
May 11	Return to London
May 12	Carmen: concert Nottingham
May 19	Carmen: concert in Hull
June 2	BBC concert RFH (met Terry Wogan)
June 13	To Santa Fe
June 14	Grand Duchess Reh. SF
June 30	Grand Duchess:
	1st night of Santa Fe Festival
July 4/6/14	Grand Duchess: SF
July 21 – Aug. 25	Returned to London twice
	In this period, returning for further perfs.
August 6/23/25	Grand Duchess in SF
September 27/28	G&S concert: BBC Reh.
Sept. 29	G&S concert BBC. RFH
October 20	Travel to Monterrey, Mexico
Oct. 25/27	Carmen: Monterrey
Oct. 28	To Guadalajara
November 5	Carmen: Guadalajara. Return London
December 10	Hansel & Gretel: Reh. ENON
Dec. 16	Max Jaffa show BBC
Dec. 18	Hansel & Gretell: sitzprobe ENON
Dec. 18/21	Hansel & Gretel: Reh.
Dec. 24	Hansel & Gretel: Dress Reh. Leeds
Dec. 29	Hansel & Gretel: 1st night Leeds

1980

January 2/4/8	Hansel & Gretel: Leeds ENON
Jan. 10	To Rouen. Carmen Reh.
Jan. 18/20	Carmen: Rouen
Jan. 28 – 31	Die Fledermaus: Reh. in German
February 1	Die Fledermaus: Reh.
Feb. 3	(Sunday) Die Fled.: concert Sadler's Wells
Feb. 8	Hansel & Gretel: Farnside
Feb. 12/15/18/19	The Ring: Reh. ENO
Feb. 13	Hansel & Gretel: Hull ENON
Feb. 20	Hansel & Gretel: Coventry
Feb. 25	Mines of Sulphur: music call Leeds ENON
March 3	Rhinegold: Bristol ENO
March 4	Valkyrie: Bristol ENO
March 5	Mines of Sulphur: Reh. ENON.Leeds
	Then return to London
March 11 – 26	Mines of S: Reh. Leeds ENON
March 27	Mines of S: 1st night Leeds ENON
March 29	Mines of S: Perf.
March 31/April 1	The Ring: Liverpool ENO
April 2	Mines of S: Leeds ENON
April 10	Carmen: sitzprobe ENON
April 15/17/19	Carmen: Glasgow ENON
April 24/26	Mines of S: Hull ENON
May 13 – 19	Television work for Mines of Sulphur
May 27	To Ghent to Reh. Sams & Del
June 7/10/13/15	Samson & Delilah: Ghent
	Then return to London

July 11	To Pretoria, South Africa	Feb. 22	L'amico Fritz: a week of rehearsals
July 12 – Aug. 12	Carmen: Reh. Pretoria	March 1	L'amico Fritz: New Jersey
August 14	Carmen: 1st night Pretoria	March 2	Elektra: Forth Worth Reh.
Aug. 16/18/20/22	Carmen: Pretoria	March 12/15	Elektra: Fort Worth
Aug. 25	To Johannesburg		Return home via Chicago
Aug. 29/Sept. 2/4/6/8/10/12		March 17 – 26	Il trovatore: learning role
	Carmen: Johannesburg	March 28	Il trovatore: 2 weeks Reh. Baltimore
	Then return to London	April 9	Il trovatore: 1st night Baltimore
October 5	To Day Samson & Delilah: Dayton	April 11/13	Il trovatore: Baltimore
Oct 18	Samson & Delilah: Toledo	April 14	Return to London
Oct. 20/2	To London/on to St Etienn to Rehearse	April 29/30	Stuart Burrows' TV show Cardiff
	Carmen	May 9	Clonter Farm: inaugural concert
Oct. 25	Carmen: St Etienne (one performance)	May 18/19	STV show for Arthur Blake with
November	Learning Don Quichotte		Norman Bailey
December 1	To Nice, France	May 31 – June 2	Concert Kenneth McKeller's show
December 5/7	Don Quichotte: Nice		Glasgow
December:	Learning Rigoletto (Maddalena) with	June	Secret Marriage: learning and rehearsing
	Tom Gligeroff	July 9	Secret Marriage: Buxton Reh.
		July 25	Secret Marriage: 1st night Buxton
1981		July 30	Secret Marriage: Buxton
		August 1/4/6/8	Secret Marriage: Buxton
January 2 – 16	Rigoletto: Reh for perf. In 1983	August 28	John Socman: Learning for BBC Radio
Jan. 14/15	Travel to Groningen to rehearse Boris	September 7 – 12	John Socman Reh. BBC Radio
	Godounov	Sept. 14 – 17	John Socman: recording Manchester
Jan. 16	Boris Godounov: Groningen	Sept. 23/25	Façade: voice-over
Jan. 17	Boris Godounov: Utrecht	October 11	Carmen: Calgary Reh.
Jan/Feb	L'amico Fritz: learning role of Beppe	Oct. 22/24/26	Carmen: Calgary
February 19	To New York		Return to London

November 16	To Beçason, France: Carmen: Reh.
Nov. 22	Carmen: Beçason
Nov. 25	Carmen: Ghent
December 12/18/20	Carmen: Antwerp
Dec. 21/28	Carmen: Bruges

1982

January 8	BBC: Friday Night is Music Night
Jan. 15	To Antwerp
Jan. 16/18/24	Carmen: Antwerp
Jan. 25	To St Etienne to Reh. Herodiade
Jan. 30	Grand Duchess: Rehs begin SW
April 28	Grand Duchess: 1st night SW
April 29/30	Grand Duchess SW
May 1	Grand Duchess: 2 perfs.
May 3 – 8	Grand Duchess: daily perfs.
June 11	BBC Friday Night Is Music Night
June 14	Ruddigore: Reh. For American TV
July 5	Trojans: Reh. For BBC Prom
July 16	The Fall Of Troy: BBC Prom
September 1	Samson & Delilah: Reh. ENON
Sept. 23/25	BBC: Bexhill Live relay of opera concert
Sept. 28/29/30	Samson & Delilah: Reh. ENON
October 4	Samson & Delilah: dress reh.
Oct. 6	Samson & Delilah: 1st night Leeds
Oct. 9	Samson & Delilah: Leeds
Oct. 14	Samson & Delilah: Manchester

Oct. 18	Le Grande Macabre: Reh. Start ENO
Oct. 19	Sams & Del: Manchester ENON
Oct. 28	Sams & Del: Nottingham ENON
November 4/6	Sams & Del: Hull ENON
November	Le Grand Macabre: regular rehearsals
December 2	Le Grand Macabre: 1st night ENO LC
Dec. 7/9/15/17/21	Le Grand Macabre: ENO LC

1983

January 2	To Avignon Reh. Rigoletto
Jan. 9/12/15	Rigoletto: Avignon
Jan. 16	Return to London
Jan 21/22	Carmen: Reh. Travel to Toledo
JAN. 29	Carmen: Toledo
	Return to London via Detroit
Jan. 31 – Feb. 25	Tristan & Isolde:
	Learning with Mary Nash
Feb. 27	Tristan & Isolde: Reh.
	To New Orleans
March 10	Trist & Isol: 1st night New Orleans
March 12	Trist & Isol: New Orleans
March 14	Return to London
March 21	Carmen: Reh. Limoges
March 26	Carmen: Limoges
March 29	The Gambler: Learning work
April 11—26	The Gambler: Rehs. ENO
May 28	The Gambler: 1st night ENO LC

May 3/6/10/14	The Gambler
May 18	The Gambler: relay for BBC from LC
May	Rehs. Carmen while The Gambler in perf.
May 24	Carmen: Dress reh. Plymouth ENO
May 26/ June 1/3/8	Carmen: Plymouth ENO
June 9	To Santa Fe
June 10	Orpheus in the Underworld: Rehs
June	Regular Rehs. Orph. Underworld
July 1	Orph. Underworld: 1st night SF
July 7/9/13/22	Orph. Underworld SF
July 16	Arabella: 1st night SF
July 20/29	Arabella: SF
August 4/9/18/23/25/27	Orph. Underworld SF
Aug. 6/11/19	Arabella: SF
August 28	Return to London
September 1	Rebecca: Rehs. Begin ENON
Sept. – Oct 13	Rebecca: ENON Leeds
	Returning home at weekends
October 15	Rebecca: world premier ENON Leeds
Oct. 18/21/26	Rebecca: Leeds ENON
	Regularly returning to London for Rehs.
November 1	Mireille: Rehs begin ENO
Nov. 4	Rebecca: Nottingham
Nov. 9	BBC concert Reh Golders Green
Nov. 11	Rebecca: Manchester
Nov. 12	Concert in Nottingham
Nov. 14 – 28	Mireille: Rehs ENO

December 1	Mireille: 1st night ENO LC
December 3/6/9/14/16/22/30	Mireille LC

1984

January 13	BBC Friday Night Is Music Night
Jan. 23	To Rouen: Carmen Reh.
Jan. 29	Carmen: matinee Rouen
Jan. 31/Feb 3/5	Carmen: Rouen Ann's final Carmen
Jan. 6 – 22	War & Peace: learning ENO
Feb. 24	BBC Friday Night Is Music Night
Feb. 27	War & Peace: Rehs. Until March 28 ENO
March 31	War & Peace: 1st night ENO LC
April 4/6/14/18	War & Peace
April 12	Rusalka: learning/Rehs ENO
May 1/3/5/8/11/16/21/23	Rusalka/ War & Peace
	Rehearsals for these two operas sometimes on same day
May 27	To Austin, Texas ENO tour
May 29	War & Peace: Dress Reh. Austin
May 31	War & Peace: 1st night Austen
June 2	War & Peace: Austen
June 3	Return to London
June 23	Re-join ENO tour in USA
June 25/26	War & Peace: Rehs. In New York Met

June 27/29	War & Peace Perfs. In New York Met
July 1	Return to London with ENO company
July 5/6	Irmelin BBC Radio London
July 23	L'Orione: Scottish Opera/ learning
August 20	L'Orione: Edinburgh Fest. Dress Reh.
August 21	L'Orione: 1st night Edinburgh SO
August 23/25	L'Orione: Edinburgh SO
September 18	To Santiago, Chile Sams.& Del.
October 2	Sams.& Del: 1st night Santiago
Oct. 4/7	Sams.& Del: Santiago
Oct. 8	Return to London
Oct. 15	Rusalka: Rehs. Begin ENO
Oct. 22/23	L'Orione: Rehs. Glasgow SO
Oct. 24	L'Orione: Perfs Glasgow SO
October 25/26	Rusalka: Reh. In London ENO
Oct. 26	(evening) To Glasgow:
Oct. 27	L'Orione: Glasgow SO
Oct. 28	L,Orione: Reh. SO
Oct. 28	Return to London
Oct. 29	Rusalka: Reh. ENO
Oct. 29	Travel back to Glasgow
Oct. 30	L'Orione: Perf. Glasgow SO
Oct. 31	To London. Rusalka: Reh.
November 1	To Glasgow: L'Orione: Perf.
Nov. 3	L'Orione: Matinee Glasgow SO
Nov. 4	Return to London. Rusalka Rehs.
	Until November 12
Nov.	15 Rusalka: 1st night ENO LC

Nov.	21/22/26/29 Rusalka: Perfs. ENO LC
December 5/8/14	Rusalka: ENO LC
	Rusalka was being recorded for TV during Perfs.

1985

January/February	Learning The Tempest
	Practice sessions with Mary Nash
March 12	To Boulogne: Carmen
May 6	To give a Master Class on last act of Carmen at Royal College of Music
May 28	Travel to Glasgow Reh. Concert prog.
May 29	Concert: Perth Scottish Nat. Orch.
June 1	Travel to Santa Fe
June 3	Santa Fe: Rehs. Orph.Underworld
June 29	Orph. Underworld: 1st night SF
July 5/10/19/30	Orph. Underworld Perfs. SF
July 27	The Tempest: 1st night SF
July 31	The Tempest: SF
August 5/8/14/20/24	Orph. Underworld SF
August 9/17	The Tempest: SF
August 25	Return to London
September/October	Learning title role of Katya Kabanova ENO
November 14	Katya Kabanova: 1st night LC
Nov. 23/28	Katya Kabanova: ENO LC
December 6/11	Katya Kabanova: ENO LC

1986

Jan/Feb/March	Il trovatore: Rehs. ENO
March 27	Concert : Barbican, London
April 3	BBC: Reh.
April 5	BBC concert: RFH
April 7 – 14	Holiday
April	Regular Rehs: Rusalka ENO
May 4	Charity concert for Hazel Vivian
June 17	Rusalka: 1st night ENO LC
June 20/25/28	Rusalka: filmed for TV
June 29	Travel to Sicily: Reh. Carmen
July 5/7	Carmen in Taormina, Sicily
July 10	Return to London
July 14	Il trovatore: Reh. ENO
	Holiday in Mallorca
August 4	Il trovatore: Rehs. ENO
Aug. 27	Il trovatore: 1st night ENO LC
Aug. 30	Il trovatore: ENO LC
September 2/5/10/12/17/20/25	
	Il trov. ENO LC
Sept. 8	BBC: Concert: Reh.
Sept. 13	BBC: Concert: Birmingham
Sept. 27	Mikado: Rehs. For ENO
October 18	Mikado: 1st night ENO LC
Oct 24/Nov 4/7/13/20/25	
	Mikado ENO LC
December 19/21	ENO Concerts

1987

January 19 – Feb. 13	Mikado Rehs. (New Coco)
Feb. 16	Mikado: 1st night of new run ENO LC
Feb. 19	Mikado ENO LC
Feb. 20/23/24/25/27	BBC: M anchester
	Reh./ Record opera
Feb. 28	Mikado: matinee/evening ENO LC
March 5/11/14/17/19/26	
	Mikado: ENO LC
March 28	Mikado: matinee/evening ENO LC
April 1/8	Mikado: ENO LC
April 10/11	BBC concert: Cardiff
April 18	Concert: Glasgow
September 18	Iolanthe: Perf. Windsor Castle
Sept. 27	Concert: Chiswick Town Hall
November 23	Rebecca: Rehs. Leeds ENON
Nov. 26	Plumber's Gift: First look ENO
December 4/5	Adriana Lecouvreur (Cilea) BBC
December	Rebecca: Rehs. In Leeds ENON

1988

January 2	Rebecca: 1st night Leeds ENON
Jan. 4/6/8	Rebecca: Leeds ENON
Feb. 25	Rebecca: Reh. (new Cast) Manchester ENON
Feb. 26	Rebecca: Manchester ENON

April 10	To Scotland		December 10	Mikado: matinee/evening Perfs.
April 11	Candide: Rehs. Glasgow SO		Dec. 15/19/21/23/30	Mikado: ENO LC
April 16/20/24	Candide: recording/ further Rehs.			
May 17	Candide: Gala preview Glasgow SO		*1989*	
May 19	Candide: Press night SO			
May 20/21	Candide: Filming for BBC TV		January 5	Mikado: ENO LC
May 24/28 June 2	Candide: Perfs. Glasgow SO		Jan. 14	Mikado: matinee/evening ENO LC
June 8	Candide: Reh. Newcastle (on tour) SO		Jan. 17/19	Mikado: ENO LC
June 9/11	Candide: Newcastle SO		Jan 21	Mikado: matinee/evening ENO LC
June 16/17	Candide: Liverpool SO		Jan. 26/Feb. 7/10	Mikado: ENO LC
June 23/24	Candide: Edinburgh SO		February/March	Plumber's Gift: Learning
June 29/July 1	Candide: Final Perfs. SO		April 10	Plumber's Gift: Reh.
July 27/28/29	Die Fledermaus: ENO LC			Regular rehearsals during April/May
July 30	Die Fled: matinee and evening		May 25	Plumber's Gift: 1st night ENO LC
	ENO LC		May 31/June 6/9/12/15	Plumber's Gift ENO LC
August 8/11	Plumber's Gift: Rehs. At LC for ENO		June/July August	Holiday in early July
Aug. 28	BBC: Reh. For G&S concert/Aldeburgh			Learning Marriage of Figaro for SO
Aug. 29	Travel to Aldeburgh		August 23	To Glasgow
Aug. 30	BBC G&S concert in Aldeburgh		August 25	M of Fig. First Reh. Glasgow SO
September 1	Plumber's Gift: Reh. London ENO		September 11	BBC concert Reh.
Sept. 12	BBC concert: Rehs. All day		Sept. 12	BBC concert RFH
Sept. 16	BBC concert RFH		Sept. 15/16	Diary reads 'Ill all day'
Sept. 22/28/29	Plumber's Gift: Reh. ENO London		Sept. – Oct. 4	M of Fig. Rehs Glasgow SO
October 4/6/12	Plumber's Gift Rehs. ENO		Oct. 5	M of Fig. 1st night Glasgow SO
	(Eventual first perf. May 1989)		Oct. 7/19/21	M of Fig. Perfs. Glasgow SO
Oct. 17 – Nov.	Mikado: Rehs. New run		Oct. 18/31	M of Fig. 'brush-up' Rehs.
Nov. 23	Mikado: 1st night ENO LC		November 1/3	M of Fig. Glasgow SO
Nov. 25/29 Dec. 1/3/8	Mikado Perfs. ENO LC		Nov. 8/10	M of Fig. Newcastle SO

Nov. 14/17	M of Fig. Aberdeen SO
Nov 27/28	M of Fig. Glasgow SO
Dec 5/7	M of Fig. Glasgow SO

1990

January 4	The Gambler: Learning ENO LC
February 5	The Gambler: Reh. Start
	Rehs. until March 12
February 22/26	Gipsy Baron: Reh. BBC
Feb. 27	Gipsy Baron: recording for BBC
March 14	The Gambler: 1st night ENO LC
March 17/22/29/3	The Gambler: ENO LC
April 3/5/10	The Gambler: ENO LC
May 3/4/9/10/14	Peter Grimes: ENO LC
	Start of long rehearsal period.
July 23/24/25/26	Into The Woods: Rehs.
August into Sept.	Into The Woods: Rehs
Sept. 14	Into The Woods
	First preview (London West End)
Sept. 25	Into The Woods: 1st night
	Following 4 to 5 months performing
	Into The Woods 8 times a week.

1991

January 14/16	In.Woods: recording
Jan 16	Peter Grimes: Reh. ENO

Feb. 27	Peter Grimes: Start of long Reh. Period
April 17	Peter Grimes: 1st night ENO LC
April 29/24/26/29	Peter Grime: ENO LC
May 2/8/16/22/25/28/31	
	P.Gr. ENO LC
June 4/10/15/18/21	P. Gr. ENO LC
July 8/11/17	Fiery Angel Reh. BBC
August 12/15	Fiery Angel REhs. BBC
Aug. 16	Fiery Angel: Manchester BBC
Aug. 21	BBC: concert Reh. Record
September	Mikado Die Fled. Rehs.
October 5	Mikado matinee ENO LC
Oct. 8/11/17/26	Mikado: Perfs. ENO LC
Nov. 14/23/24	Royal Variety Show Rehs.

1992

Jan. 3/8/11/15/18/28	Die Fled. ENO LC
Feb. 1/6/10	Die Fled. ENO LC
March 31	P. Gr. Reh. For concert Perf.
April 6	Boris Godounov: Reh. In Leeds ENON
April 21	ENO concert St Martin-in-the Fields
May 16	Boris G. 1st night Leeds ENON
May 20/23	Boris G. Nottingham ENON
May 27/29	Boris G. Manchester ENON
June 1/3/5	Boris G. Leeds ENON
June 10/13	Boris G. Sheffield ENON
June 19	Concert in Belfast: Donald Maxwell

July 8	BBC: discussion/quiz programme
Sept. 5	Boris G. Reh. Leeds for BBC Prom.
Sept. 8	Boris G. BBC Prom RAH

1993

January 3	Concert: Greenwich. for Mark Tinkler to
	promote Pocket Opera
April 22	Covent Garden to Reh. Concert
April 23	Concert: ROH to sing
	'People who need people'
May 2 – 14	In New York/holiday
May 28/29	Concert in Warrington
July 13/14/15	Elektra Rehs.
July 16	Elektra: (excerpts) BBC Prom
August 6	Salome: Reh. BBC Prom
August 7	Salome: BBC Prom RAH
November 21	Brief visit to Munich
Nov 26	BBC: Friday Night Is Music Night
Nov. 28	To Munich Reh. P. Gr.
Dec 13/16/19/22	P. Gr. Munich

1994

Jan. 3/4 and 8/12	P.Gr. Munich
	Returning to London in between
Feb/March	Teaching: Private practice
April 11	P.Gr. Reh. for TV ENO

April/May	P.Gr. Rehs.
May 20	P.Gr. 1st night ENO LC
May 25/27	P.Gr. ENO LC
June 2/4/7/10/14/16	P.Gr. ENO LC
June 19	P.Gr. Special Reh. for TV
June 21/24/27/30	P.Gr. Perfs. For TV
July 4	To New York Reh. HMS Pinafore
July 23	HMS Pin. 1st night Purchase
July 24	HMS Pin.. matinee Purchase
October 5	To Lisbon Reh. Candide
	For staged concert Perf.
Oct. 12/14/16	Candide: Lisbon
Nov. 20	To New York Reh. P.Gr Met
Dec. 12	P.Gr. 1st night NY Met
Dec. 15/19/23/28	P.Gr. NY Met
Dec. 31	P.Gr. Matinee NY Met

1995

January 3	P.Gr. Last Perf. NY Met
Jan. 4	Return to London
	(Diary illustrated with bells and fireworks
	'Hurray')

Following months: Work on Sancta Susanna for concerts in
Barbican and RAH. Also work on Street Scene for Perf. in
Portugal in May and June. To Turin for Street Scene in December

1996

	Doctor of Myddfai for Welsh National Opera
Sept.	Iolanthe: Purchase USA
Nov.	The Mikado: new run ENO LC

1997

January	Mikado until Jan 18 ENO LC
Feb. 16	To Munich Reh. P.Gr. ENO production with new singers. International cast. Bayerische Staatsoper
March 1	P.Gr. 1st night Munich
March 5/9/12	P.Gr. Perfs. in Munich
September.	Return to Munich
Sept. 28, Oct. 1/5/9	P.Gr. Munich

1998

January 14	To Munich Reh. P.Gr.
Jan. 18	P.Gr. 1st night Munich
Jan' 22/26/30	P.Gr .Munich
	Returning home between Perfs.
Oct/Nov.	To Vienna P.Gr. New production

1999

Ann's last year of professional singing: Peter Grimes with Welsh National Opera.

INDEX

ABOUT THE AUTHOR

Susan Higgins has had a wide-ranging career in music which has included music journalism. She studied at the Arts Centre, Dartington Hall, and trained as a singer at the Guildhall School of Music and Drama in London with Walther Gruner. A solo singing career followed, giving two well-received recitals in the Wigmore Hall, broadcasting for BBC Radio 3 and singing in oratorio and opera.

She subsequently developed a busy practice, teaching violin, viola and piano as well as singing. In recent years her solo singing work has been replaced with conducting. She works with choral societies and choirs and has performed a great deal of the choral repertoire. She also runs a Singers' Workshop.

She first met Ann Howard (who is fortuitously a neighbour in Surbiton) when she received a series of voice lessons to introduce her to the mezzo-soprano range and repertoire. Ann, using her Modesti voice techniques, encouraged Susan to have a second career as a solo singer.

Writing started by working for Rhinegold Publishing. She made regular contributions to Classical Music', 'Music Teacher', and 'The Singer' and at one time produced a music newspaper in Surrey.

She is married to fellow musician Tom Higgins who, for many years, played in the orchestra of English National Opera. He often travelled to the Coliseum on the train with Ann. He subsequently embarked on a busy and successful career as a conductor and arranger. They have two grown-up children.

Lightning Source UK Ltd.
Milton Keynes UK
UKOW06f2340050214

225980UK00006B/15/P